DEFINING THE MOMENT OF DEATH: BRAIN DEATH IN INDIA AND THE UNITED STATES

ANAMIKA KRISHNAN

notionpress.com

INDIA • SINGAPORE • MALAYSIA

ISBN
Paperback 979-8-89556-327-4
Hardcase 979-8-89610-329-5

DEFINING THE MOMENT OF DEATH: A CRITICAL AND COMPARATIVE ANALYSIS OF THE ETHICS AND LEGAL FRAMEWORKS GOVERNING BRAIN DEATH IN INDIA AND THE UNITED STATES

*Excerpts from the dissertation submitted to the Faculty of Robert H. McKinney School of Law in partial fulfillment of the requirements for the degree Master of Laws (LL.M.) in Health Law, Policy, and Bioethics, July 2023

Indiana University – Purdue University Indianapolis

DEDICATION

As I rewrite the initial dedication page today, life has surprised me with another full circle moment. I have a full-time job, immigration papers, and now I'm part of one of the most prestigious leadership cohorts in Indiana.

I remember the chaos that I went through when I moved to the United States all alone. I did not know a single human being in Indiana. When I thought I had gained a grip over my life's course, systemic and institutional racism threw me off the tracks. There has not been a single day when I was a student that I did not want to go back to my homeland. I remember the tears, sweat, pain, and agony that I went through to research this niche-area of bioethics. Most of my days and nights were spent at the libraries. Writing a thesis on law and medicine, while the medical bills were drowning me in debts, seemed to be ironic. But I survived. I survived for my ancestors, who were uneducated landless laborers. I survived for my grandmother who instilled the notion of social justice in me. I survived for my parents who are my backbone. I survived for my partner who made sure that I did not starve to death. I survived for our future generations, who will, hopefully have the support and power to fight back the system. I survived capitalism, medical racism, and accent discrimination. I survived, and I'm resilient, and I refuse to back down.

I dedicate this book to every immigrant in the United States, who are the embodiment of resilience and faith. I believe in your dreams and abilities. You are the future.

CONTENTS

ABSTRACT

This book addresses the complexities and the ethical and legal concerns surrounding determination of brain death in India and U.S.A. Brain death is a highly contested issue and in the recent times, there have been several attempts to limit declaring brain death as biological death in both the countries. Lack of awareness, cultural and religious beliefs, and decline in the belief of scientific reasoning and logic are some of the major reasons for this setback. Both the countries are equally equipped with the legislative power to enact or modify existing laws to overcome these challenges. This research project attempts to analyze why brain death should be considered death and break down legal and ethical arguments against this determination and rebut them. It also compares the legal frameworks and ethical guidelines of both the countries and identifies key developments in the 21st century that may serve as a yardstick for them to revisit and review their approach to the issue. There are principles and ideas that they can learn from each other. However, the researcher also pays meticulous attention to the differences in the legal systems and the social fabrics of the countries.

"The biggest weapon wielded and actually daily unleashed by imperialism against that collective defiance is the cultural bomb. The effect of a cultural bomb is to annihilate a people's belief in their names, in their languages, in their environment, in their heritage of struggle, in their unity, in their capacities and ultimately in themselves."

~ Ngũgĩ wa Thiong'o

Here's to remembering our heritage, our ancestors, and rediscovering ourselves.

AUTHOR'S NOTE

> *"To conquer the empire, we must begin with the liberation of our own minds from the colonial legacy."*
>
> – *Nicolás Guillén*

When we talk about medical advancements, why do we immediately picture a European nation and think of scientists as White? At the same time, why do our subconscious minds associate poverty and violence primarily with the global South? Violence is often defined only in physical terms, but when millions are denied insurance coverage and are on the brink of bankruptcy, what should we call that? What exactly is violence?

Why do I not see people like me in clinical trials? Why do you complain about my hormones, while constantly undermine and underfund research into endometriosis?

When tasked with writing a 100-page thesis on brain death, many assumed it would be a boring, non-linear exploration of science and law. However, the society in which science exists is complex and multifarious. Brain death is thus not a black-and-white topic. This work is a humble attempt to read bioethics and brain death through the lenses of racial justice and health equity. Instead of comparing the U.S. with any European country, I chose to write about Kerala, my homeland, which boasts the highest life expectancy and Human Development Index in India. I talk about what the United States can learn from Kerala.

This is my protest, and the collective protest of colonized people. The work explores the history of colonization of bioethics and medicine, how imperialism has supported the paternalistic approach of science, and the ongoing struggle to reclaim collective power for systemically oppressed communities.

With solidarity,

Anamika Krishnan

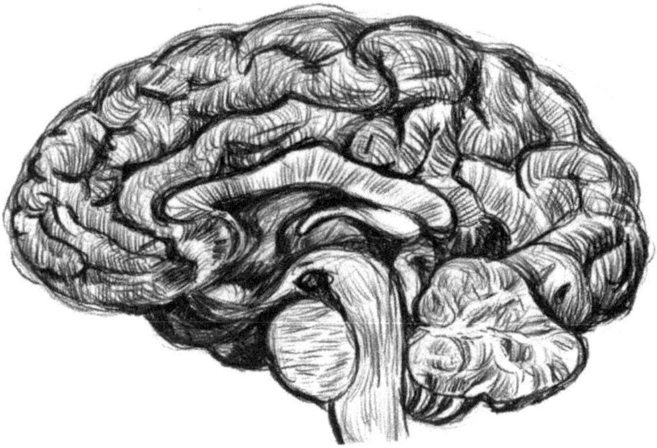

Illustration Courtesy: *Aswath C. (India)*

CHAPTER

01

LIFE, DEATH, AND BRAIN DEATH: OUTLINING THE MEDICAL HISTORY

"The boundaries which divide life from death are at best shadowy and vague.

Who shall say where the one ends, and where the other begins?"[1]

The varying definitions of life and death in philosophy, science, law, and religions have led to numerous conflicts and controversies. Ethical questions about life have baffled lawmakers and the medical community for many centuries. Some of these questions revolve around the concept of life, its beginning, meaning, significance, and the end. Even though life and death are distinct universal truths, they cannot be defined independently. Death must be studied and explored in the context of life as it is the cessation of life.[2] To make this inquiry even more complex, life is susceptible to distinct definitions depending on the context. Life is the quality that differentiates a vital and functional

---

[1] EDGAR ALLAN POE, POETRY AND TALES: THE PREMATURE BURIAL (Patrick F. Quinn ed., Library of America 1984) (1844).
[2] Thomas v. Anderson, 96 Cal. App. 2d 371 (1950).

being from a corpse.[3] It is the state of a coordinated being in which its essential functions and motions are performed.[4]

A question may arise in the present context on whether Artificial Intelligence (AI) qualifies to be life. What distinguishes AI from biological life is the ability to grow, reproduce, and continually change. AI does not grow, reproduce, or change biologically, rather it is the human factor that alters it. In simple terms, the existence of cells and genetic material differentiates living beings from AI. Life may be defined as a feature that distinguishes living and non-living matter or an attribute of something that defends its existence in the environment.[5] Life may also be defined as an open mechanism that utilizes gradients in the environment to replicate[6], or a self-supported chemical arrangement adequate to undergo Darwinian evolution[7], or a structure sustained by information, energy, and matter.[8] Plato defined life as the realization of the highest

---

[3] MERRIAM WEBSTER DICTIONARY (12th ed. 2022)

[4] BLACK'S LAW DICTIONARY (11th ed. 2019).

[5] Chris P. McKay, *What is Life and How Do We Search for It in Other Worlds?*, 2(9) PLoS Biol. 1261, 1260-1263 (2004) (discussing comparable patterns in the organics of life on earth and space).

[6] H. Lammer et al., *What Makes a Planet Habitable?*, 17(2) Astron. Astrophys Rev. 181-249 (2009) (discussing the connection of life to habitability).

[7] DAVID W. DEAMER & GAIL R. FLEISCHAKER, ORIGINS OF LIFE: THE CENTRAL CONCEPTS (1994) (summarizing the suggestion of Carl Sagan to redefine life in the cosmos).

[8] Nedilkjo Budisa, *Xenobiology: A Journey Towards Parallel Life Forms*, 21 ChemBioChem., 2229, 2228-2231 (2020).

form of oneself.[9] Descartes viewed it as a form of self-movement, continuation, or self-modification.[10] Kant identified life as the faculty of a being to act as per the laws of the faculty of desire[11] while Nietzsche defined it as the capacity to conceive values useful to society.[12] It has been also held that life does not mean a merely breathing animal, but the ability to live with dignity. The right to life envelops all those components of life that make a man's life significant and whole.[13]

Death is defined by physicians as the absolute termination of the circulation of blood and other vital functions.[14] The father of modern histology wrote that life is the ensemble of functions that resist death.[15] Thus, death would be the opposite condition of life. But defining death has been a controversy. It is a concept that has traveled in radically contrasting paths before the onset of modern science. There was no unanimity in the medical community about when life ends. Further, death would differ as per religious and cultural contexts. As per biblical

---

[9] David Skrbina, *Plato and the Meaning of Life*, in THE MEANING OF LIFE AND THE GREAT PHILOSOPHERS 8 (Stephen Leach ed., 2018).

[10] Sarah Byers, *Life as Self Motion: Descartes and The Aristotelians on the Soul as the Life of the Body*, 59 Rev. Metaphys. 723-755 (2006).

[11] IMMANUEL KANT, CRITIQUE OF PRACTICAL REASON (Lewis White Beck trans., The Bobbs-Merrill 1956) (1788).

[12] FRIEDRICH WILHELM NIETZSCHE, THUS SPOKE ZARATHUSTRA: A BOOK FOR ALL AND NONE (Walter Kaufmann trans., Modern Library 1995) (1883).

[13] Maneka Gandhi v. Union of India, AIR 1978 SC 597 (Ind.).

[14] *See supra* note 4.

[15] XAVIER BICHAT, PHYSIOLOGICAL RESEARCH ON LIFE AND DEATH (Tobias Watkins trans., Smith & Maxwell 1809) (1799).

scriptures, death is a spiritual event in which the spirit or soul departs the body.[16] The Catholic belief is that there is no precise form of death. If the heart, lungs, or brain cease to work, it does not indicate different deaths, but different forms of death.[17] Judaism views death as the absence of breathing and heartbeat.[18] In Islam, death is defined as the moment when the soul potentially leaves the body. But there is no accurate definition provided in the scriptures to determine when this moment exactly occurs.[19]

In Buddhism, death is the advancing termination of activity of five bio-dynamic forces, including digestion, ability to breathe and think clearly, excretion, and movement.[20] In Hinduism, death is the cessation of the ability to breathe.[21] In some religions like Jainism, death is an ongoing process,

---

[16] Anderson J.K., *A Biblical Appraisal of Euthanasia*, in LIVING ETHICALLY IN THE 90s 198-201 (Anderson J.K. ed., 1990).

[17] Estol C.J., *To Live and Let Die: A Brain Death Symposium at the Pontifical Academy of Science*, 2(3) Int. J Stroke. 227, 227-229 (2007) (discussing the modern Christian view articulated by Pope Benedict XVI).

[18] Fred Rosner, *The Definition of Death in Jewish Law*, in THE DEFINITION OF DEATH: CONTEMPORARY CONTROVERSIES 210-215 (Stuart Youngner et al. ed., 1999).

[19] Khan F.A., *The Definition of Death in Islam: Can Brain Death be Used as a Criteria of Death in Islam?*, 18 JAMA. 18, 18-21 (1986) (discussing the absence of a precise definition of departure of soul in Quran).

[20] Ken Holmes, *Buddhism and Death*, KAGYU SAMYE LING BLOG (Jan. 3, 2023, 3:41 AM), https://www.samyeling.org/buddhism-and-meditation/teaching-archive-2/dharmacharya-ken-holmes/buddhism-and-death/.

[21] BRITANNICA, https://www.britannica.com (last visited Dec. 11, 2022).

and the members practice a ritual called Santhara[22] where the people impending death or people who cannot consume food through mouth would stop eating to hasten death and to die with dignity. In contrast, the Catholic Church holds that tube feeding is considered morally obligatory when a patient cannot eat or drink.[23] These diverse views reflect that death is a highly sensitive subject.

Earlier, death was determined solely by cardiopulmonary and respiratory criteria.[24] If a person had stopped normal breathing, or her heart stopped beating on its own, she was considered dead. In the early 18th century, materialists and their Soviet counterparts began to view suspended animation as a curable form of death and resuscitation using chest compression techniques was considered resurrection from death, but the Western scientists viewed death as final.[25] In the 1960s, the genesis of Cardiopulmonary Resuscitation (hereinafter referred to as CPR) revolutionized modern medicine. This emergency method blends chest compressions and artificial ventilation. This is done in order to

---

[22] Julie McCarthy, *Fasting to the Death: Is it a Religious Rite or Suicide?* NPR (Sep. 2, 2015, 5:20 AM), https://www.npr.org/sections/goatsandsoda/2015/09/02/436820789/fasting-to-the-death-is-it-a-religious-rite-or-suicide.

[23] Peter Beaulieu, *When to Recommend a PEG Tube? A Decision Tree for Clinicians from a Catholic Perspective*, 79 Linacre Q. 25, 25-26 (2012).

[24] Irving S. Wright, *Who Should Make the Decisions?* in THE MOMENT OF DEATH 3, 4 (Arthur Winter ed., 1969) (discussing traditional criteria for determination of death).

[25] Martin S. Pernick, *Brain Death in a Cultural Context: The Reconstruction of Death*, in *supra* note 17.

reestablish blood circulation and breathing in an individual who endured a cardiac capture or halted breathing.[26]

At first, the key question was whether the essence of life resides in a single organ.[27] If this were the case, a person would be dead if any of the biological organs fail. But the organ transplant altered the concepts of life and death. In 1967, Louis Washkansky received the first human heart transplant in the world[28], and proved that a human could survive without an actual heart briefly during the process of transplants, where an artificial pump would manage the circulation of blood in the patient. These modern interventions rattled the traditional criteria to determine death as people could be saved from life-threatening injuries and trauma and these standards no longer were sufficient to define the exact moment of death. Around the same time, two leading French neurologists published a historically significant article[29] explaining the need to redefine

---

[26] Dianne L. Atkins, Stuart Berger, et al., *Pediatric Life Support and Cardiopulmonary Resuscitation Quality: 2015 American Heart Association Guidelines Update for CPR and Emergency Cardiovascular Care*, 132 Circ. J. 519, 525 (2015).

[27] Pernick M.S., *Back from the Grave: Recurring Controversies Over Defining and Diagnosing Death in History*, in DEATH: BEYOND WHOLE-BRAIN CRITERIA 17-24 (Zaner R.M. ed., 1988) (discussing two essential questions in determining death; whether life can be limited to the functioning of one organ and how can we avoid the inaccurate diagnosis of death).

[28] DONALD MCRAE, EVERY SECOND COUNTS: THE RACE TO TRANSPLANT THE FIRST HUMAN HEART 4 (2006).

[29] Mollaret P. & Goulon M., *Le Coma Depasse*, 101 Rev. Neurol. 3, 15 (1959).

death as per neurologic standards. They presented over two dozen clinical cases of irretrievable coma due to traumatic brain injury and argued that those patients who lost their entire cognitive and vegetative functions should be considered dead. *Coma depasse* or irreversible coma was indicated by the immobility of pupils, absence of key reflexes and motor responses to any stimuli, a flat electroencephalogram (EEG), and hypothermia or hyperthermia.[30] All these events sparked debates and dialogues on the need to redefine the criteria to determine death worldwide.

In 1968, an ad hoc committee at Harvard Medical School began to explore redefinition of irreversible coma as a criterion for death.[31] The report of the committee listed the features of irreversible coma, which are unreceptivity, unresponsiveness, absence of movements or breathing or reflexes, and a flat EEG. The report argued that if a person who suffered traumatic brain injury showed these symptoms even after repeated confirmatory tests, she should be declared dead as the condition is scientifically irreversible. This report was the first major development in the argument of construing brain death as death. In 1981, a Presidential Commission published a report[32] on defining death

---

[30] *Id.*

[31] *A Definition of Irreversible Coma: Report of the Ad Hoc Committee of the Harvard Medical School to Examine the Definition of Brain Death*, JAMA., 205, 337-340 (1968).

[32] PRESIDENT'S COMMISSION FOR THE STUDY OF ETHICAL PROBLEMS IN MEDICINE AND BIOMEDICAL AND BEHAVIORAL

and adopted the whole-brain death criteria as the standard of death. Thereafter, whole brain death criteria were adopted as a standard to determine death in the United States and many European countries. A person who sustained termination either of circulatory or respiratory functions, or irreversible functions of the entire brain, including the brain stem, began to be considered as dead.[33] Even though brain death benefited and popularized organ transplantation, it evolved independently due to the advancements in emergency medical care.[34]

Brain death has been characterized as the ultimate stoppage of movement within the central nervous system, particularly as demonstrated by a flat-level EEG for a predetermined period of time.[35] This idea suggests that brain death is not declared impromptu. Determining death by brain death criteria requires rigorous clinical standards and technological confirmatory tests. The clinical criteria to determine brain death rest on three cardinal anomalies, namely, severe coma of a known cause, absence of brainstem function or reflexes, and sustained apnea. Apnea is a disorder where breathing stops in an unconscious state and the

---

RESEARCH, DEFINING DEATH: MEDICAL, LEGAL AND ETHICAL ISSUES IN THE DETERMINATION OF DEATH (1981).

[33] ULC, UNIFORM DETERMINATION OF DEATH ACT (1981).

[34] Calixto Machado et al., The Concept of Brain Death did not Evolve to Benefit Organ Transplants, 33 J Med Ethics., 197-200 (2007).

[35] *See supra note* 4.

muscles of inhalation within the lungs stop moving.[36] The confirmatory tests are EEG[37], arteriography[38], and transcranial doppler ultrasonography.[39] So, first the physicians must determine whether the patient is in a coma. This can be confirmed by checking for no eye movement or reflex in the body to pain.[40] The physicians and neurologists must perform physical examination thoroughly to complete central pain assessment.[41] If coma and absence of brainstem reflex are confirmed, the apnea test must be performed. The patient will be briefly removed from artificial ventilation and checked for the ability to breathe spontaneously.[42] If after ten minutes, no breathing is noticed and the blood carbon dioxide levels drop fatally, the patient meets the criteria for brain death.[43] If the patient cannot be subjected to apnea test, other ancillary tests shall be performed.

The scientific inquiry into brain death has multifarious connotations. In the early 1990s, scientists began to explore how much of the brain

---

[36] NATIONAL HEALTH SERVICES, https://www.nhs.uk (last visited Dec. 24, 2022).

[37] Hughes J.R., *Limitations of the EEG in Coma and Brain Death*, 315 Ann. NY Acad Sci. 121-136 (1978).

[38] Greitz T. et al., *Aortocranial and Carotid Angiography in Determination of Brain Death*, 5 Neurorad. 13-19 (1973).

[39] Aasled R. et al., *Noninvasive Transcranial Doppler Ultrasound Recording of Flow Velocity in Basal Cerebral Arteries*, 57 J. Neurosurg. 769-774 (1982).

[40] Kristin Walter, *Brain Death*, 324 JAMA 1116 (2020).

[41] Aboubakr M. et al., *Brain Death Criteria*, NIH (Nov. 27, 2022, 9:00 AM), https://www.ncbi.nlm.nih.gov/books/NBK545144/

[42] Calixto Machado et al., *Brain Death Diagnosis and Apnea Test Safety*, 12 Ann Indian Acad Neurol., 197-200 (2009).

[43] *See supra note* 39.

must be dead to legally declare death. They have not yet found a definitive answer to this question. Although most physicians still follow the whole brain death criteria, some scholars have pointed out certain scientifically sound and evidence-based arguments to highlight the drawbacks of this approach. The whole brain cannot die as long as there is some kind of electrical activity generated inside the skull even if it is just a hormone secretion from the pituitary gland.[44] The Royal College of Physicians argued that death could be determined by the irreversible loss of brainstem function alone.[45] Their report asserted that death involves the permanent loss of fundamental features required for human existence and that death is the irreversible loss of the capacity for consciousness, and the loss of the ability to breathe.[46]

In 2008, the majority of the President's Council was of the opinion that death could be declared if an organism loses its capacity to perform the vital functions, in particular, the respiratory activity combined with the loss of brain function.[47] Recently, a team of renowned bioethicists published a work[48] arguing that death should be determined through a

---

[44] Halevy A & Broody B, *Brain Death: Reconciling Definitions, Criteria, and Tests*, 119 Ann Intern Med. 519-525 (1993).

[45] *Criteria for the Diagnosis of Brainstem Death*, 29 J R Coll. Physicians Lond. 381-382 (1995).

[46] *Id.*

[47] THE PRESIDENT'S COUNCIL ON BIOETHICS, CONTROVERSIES IN THE DETERMINATION OF DEATH: A WHITE PAPER (2008).

[48] Arthur L. Caplan et al., *Revise the Uniform Determination of Death Act to Align the Law with Practice Through Neurorespiratory Criteria*, 98

neurorespiratory criterion, whereby death would be declared if the brain injury leads to the changeless loss of capacity for consciousness, capacity to breathe spontaneously, and brainstem reflexes. Thus, the concept of brain death has an unprecedented history, and the concept is still evolving with the advancements in science and technology.

Neurol. 532-536 (2022) (discussing the advantages of neurorespiratory criteria to determine death).

***Illustration Courtesy:** Aswath C. (India)*

CHAPTER

02

MAPPING THE LEGAL HISTORY OF BRAIN DEATH ACROSS THE WORLD

Death is multidimensional. It has several philosophical and legal implications. However, it is not easy to determine the exact occurrence of life and death in the multitude of philosophies, medical advancements, and beliefs. It is even more difficult to determine if life and death should be defined as processes or momentary events. Either of these approaches have significant medico-legal ramifications. Construing life and death as ongoing processes often leads to chaos in the legal realm. A renowned American philosopher once opined that death originates with the dawn of life as the body continuously cascades and replaces perished biological materials.[49] But if this response were to be adopted as the legal definition of death, we would all be already in the dying process which may cause legal entanglements.

We are in the dying process, philosophically and biologically. But adopting this notion in the legal

[49] Ronald M. Green, *Toward a Copernican Revolution in Our Thinking About Life's Beginning and Life's End*, 66 SOUNDINGS 152, 152-162 (1983) (noting the significance of cell death: for every neuron which survives, six may die)

parlance has bad consequences. For instance, a life insurance corporation pays the death benefit to the beneficiaries of the insured upon her death. If death is defined as a process, then the insured may have started to die when she started to depend on life-support completely after a traumatic brain injury. But if she retrieves important life functions eventually, it would be a folly for the insurer to disburse the money prior to her recovery. The insurer would not pay out the money until the patient is considered legally dead, because the focus is not on the dying process but rather the moment when it occurs.

Similarly, at death, marital and parental obligations lapse, property rights of the survivors and successors emerge, and questions of organ donation arise. The best way to solve the legal quandary is to define them as instants or moments. A bilinear assortment of life and death would be the better option.[50] This idea would clarify a person's current legal status. It is imperative to draw a line between life and death, even if it is blurred. This will bring forth clarity in the legal contexts and foster transparent organ donations and optimal allocation of resources in critical care settings. This predicament is what primarily encouraged nations to introduce legal definitions of death. The acceptance of the concept of brain death did not occur in a vacuum. The declaration of death debates emerged in the

---

[50] Kirsten Rabe Smolensky, *Defining Life from the Perspective of Death: An Introduction to the Forced Symmetry Approach*, 41 U Chi Legal. 44, 41-86 (2006) (suggesting a symmetric understanding of life and death).

realm of allocating resources in intensive care and the development of transplant medicine.[51][52]

United Kingdom

Before the dawn of neurological criteria of death, U.K. followed the cardiopulmonary criteria to determine death. This longstanding approach was frustrated by the advancements in medical technology surrounding artificial ventilation.[53] The first official report on brain death was published in 1976[54] wherein methods for the diagnosis of brain death were discussed. However, this document remained silent as to whether brain death is death. It only mentioned that patients diagnosed with brain death may not recover. The second key report was published in 1979[55] and no change was made to the diagnostic protocol. It asserted that brain death denotes a stage at which a patient becomes definitively dead. The third relevant report was

---

[51] Youngner S.J., Landefeld C.S., et al. *Brain Death and Organ Retrieval: A Cross-Sectional Survey of Knowledge and Concepts among Health Professionals*, 15 JAMA 2205, 2206-2208 (1989).

[52] PETER MCCULLAGH, BRAIN DEAD, BRAIN ABSENT, BRAIN DONORS: HUMAN SUBJECTS OR HUMAN OBJECTS? (1st ed. 1993).

[53] David Albert Jones, *The UK Definition of Death*, 140 LAW & Just. – Christian L. REV. 56, 57 (1999).

[54] *Diagnosis of Brain Death: Statement issued by the Honorary Secretary of the Conference of Medical Royal Colleges and their Faculties in the United Kingdom on 11 October 1976*, 2 Br. Med J. 1187, 1187-1188 (1976).

[55] *Diagnosis of Death: Memorandum issued by the Honorary Secretary of the Conference of Medical Royal Colleges and their Faculties in the United Kingdom on 15 January 1979*, 2 Br. Med J. 332 (1979).

published in 1995[56] and the document embraced the use of the term, "brain stem death" rather than brain death. It put forth a detailed definition of death and explained why brain death implies death.[57]

As of 2023, there is still no uniform legal definition of death in the U.K. Determination of death criteria has been codified[58] and this serves as the prevailing legal standard. No legislation adopts this code, rather few cases[59] endorsed this code. Life-sustaining treatment can be withdrawn when the permanent loss of capacity for consciousness and bodily integration of biological functions is confirmed.[60] U.K. has a secular definition of death adopted by the courts, which does not allow for religious or moral exemptions. In a recent case[61], the High Court of England and Wales held that ventilation needed to be removed to allow dignity in death when a child's brain-stem tests confirmed death. The court equated brain-stem death as death, referring to the original common law ruling.[62] However, the mechanical ventilation was ordered to

---

[56] *Criteria for the Diagnosis of Brainstem Death*, 29 J R Coll. Physicians Lond. 381-382 (1995).

[57] *Id.*

[58] Peter Simpson, David Bates et. al., *A Code of Practice for the Diagnosis and Confirmation of Death: 2008*, AMRC, https://www.aomrc.org.uk/reports-guidance/ukdec-reports-and-guidance/code-practice-diagnosis-confirmation-death/.

[59] R v. Malcherek and R v. Steel, [1981] 1 WLR 690; Re A (A Minor) [1992] 3 Medical Law Reports 303 (Eng.).

[60] *Id.*

[61] Re A (A Child) [2015] EWHC 443 (Fam) (Eng.).

[62] Re A (A Minor) [1992] 3 Medical Law Reports 303 (Eng.).

be removed rejecting the parental religious objection to brain-stem death determination. This judgment once again raised several ethical questions regarding the secular definition of death in the U.K. Some legal scholars argue that the secular definition violates the moral commitment of a pluralistic society to recognize and uphold divergent religious tenets.[63] There are also arguments that the Code of Practice is outdated as it does not require the mandatory performance of confirmatory tests including EEG.[64]

Canada

Canada does not have a uniform legal definition of death. Some provinces have their own definitions of death to facilitate organ transplantation. One province defines dying as the non-reversible termination of the functioning of the organism as determined with the aid of the complete lack of the brain's capability to govern and co-ordinate all the crucial functions of the organism.[65] The tests to determine brain death are codified.[66] This response tends to restrict the scope of novel interventions in science. To address this problem, most of the

[63] Kartina A. Choong, M.Y. Rady et. al., *Re A (A Child) and the United Kingdom Code of Practice for the Diagnosis and Confirmation of Death: Should a Secular Construct of Death Override Religious Values in a Pluralistic Society?* 30 HEC Forum. 71, 71-89 (2018) (comparing the secular construct in U.K. to the UDDA in U.S.A.).

[64] *Id.*

[65] Human Organ and Tissue Donation Act, SNS 2010, Section 2(j) (Can.).

[66] Sam D. Shemie et. al., *Severe Brain Injury to Neurological Determination of Death: Canadian Forum Recommendations*, 51 CMAJ 174 (2006).

legislative provisions adopt the standard of accepted medical practice to determine brain death.[67] The courts determine the current standard of practice through case laws, from time to time. This practice allows the law to keep up with the innovations and discoveries in medicine.

Historically, the legal definition of death was based on the termination of pulse and breathing. But recent judgments have accepted neurological criteria to determine death.[68] In another case[69], the court acknowledged the imperfection in the scientific concept of brain death and the belief that death is more than just a medical phenomenon. The courts in Canada have explicitly denied applying brain death in the criminal law context, holding that it may be applicable in civil law.[70] It has been held that in order to equate brain death as death, there must be total brain death and not just the cessation of cerebral cortex activity.[71] A recent decision[72] reestablished attention to the lack of a uniform definition of death in the country. This decision portrayed an opportunity for future litigants to challenge the prevalent definition of death which is based on religious beliefs.

---

[67] Erika Chamberlain, *McKitty v. Hayani: Time for Canada to Clarify its Legal Definition of Death*, 14 MCGILL J.L. & HEALTH 219, 224 (2021).
[68] Kerr Estate v. BC Motorist Insurance Co. [1972] 6 WWR 400 (BCSC); Johannisse v. Johannisse Estate [1985] OJ No. 1273 (QL) (H Ct J) (Can.).
[69] R v. Kitching and Adams [1976] 6 WWR 697 (MBCA) (Can.).
[70] R v. Green [1988] BCJ No. 1807 (BCSC) (Can.).
[71] Leclerc (Succession) v. Turmel [2005] RJQ 1165 (SC) (Can.).
[72] McKitty v. Hayani, 2019 ONCA 805 (Can.).

The Eastern Part of the World

The concept of brain death was popularized in the Asian continent towards the end of the twentieth century. However, many countries have refrained from including brain death into medical, social, and legal domains.[73] Japan was one among the countries that opposed the concept of brain death for a long time due to cultural and religious factors.[74] There was no legal basis for brain death back in 1968[75] and organ transplant was considered as a barbarous medical experimentation.[76] The surgeon who performed the first heart transplant from a brain-dead donor in Japan was charged with the double murder of the organ donor.[77] This shocking backlash silenced the public and medical community for several years.[78] Even though there was several discussions and debates surrounding brain death and organ transplants, the fear of criminal liability stopped physicians from declaring brain death or retrieving organs. Twenty years later, the Japan

---

[73] Yang, Qing, and Geoffrey Miller, *East–west differences in Perception of Brain Death: Review of History, Current Understandings and Directions for Future Research* 8 JBI (2014).

[74] David Forster, *When the Body is Soul: The Proposed Japanese Bill on Organ Transplantations from Brain Dead Donors*, 3 PAC. RIM L.& POL'Y J. 103, 105 (1994).

[75] Michael A. Lev, *Amid a Need for Organ Donors, Japan Debates Brain Death: Two Bills Challenge Spiritual Belief*, CHICAGO TRIBUNE, Apr. 15, 1997, at 5.

[76] *See supra Note.* 73, at 121.

[77] H. Richard Beresford, *Book Review*, 27 N.Y.L. SCH. L.R. U.L.A. 593, 17, 30-31 (1982).

[78] Akira Akayabashi, *Japanese Parliament Passes Brain-Death Law*, 349 LANCET 1895, 1895 (1997).

Medical Association adopted the concept of brain death.[79] The Organ Transplant Act came into effect in late 1997, but it is narrowly worded and allows the family to veto the brain death diagnosis.[80] So, the organ transplantation law was enacted 29 years after the first organ transplant in Japan due to the conservative approach that prevails in the East and the fear of organ trafficking.

In China, the legalization of brain death has been ineffectually attempted several times.[81] Singapore has a Human Organ Transplant Act that defines brain death and sets forth strict clinical criteria to determine the same.[82] Not obtaining approval from family members is the most reported reason why brain death determination is not performed in Malaysia.[83]

In countries where most of the population follows Islam, there is widespread religious and legal disharmony surrounding brain death. As per Quran, if a person breathes air, she is considered

---

[79] ORGAN TRANSPLANTATION: MEANINGS AND REALITIES 9, 13 (Stuart J. Younger et, al., eds., 1996).

[80] *Organ Transplants Face Tough Going in Japan Despite Legislation, Cultural and Religious Beliefs Cause Obstacles*, ROCKY MOUNTAIN NEWS, Oct. 19, 1997, at 4.

[81] Yang Q., Fan Y., et al., *Acceptance in Theory but not Practice: Chinese Medical Providers' Perception of Brain Death*, 8 Neuroethics, 299, 299-313 (2015).

[82] GOVERNMENT OF SINGAPORE: WHAT IS HOTA ALL ABOUT? (2013) https://www.gov.sg/article/what-is-hota-all-about.

[83] Zaidani Attamimi, Hafizuddin Awang, et. al., *Challenges and Barriers of Brain Death Reporting in Malaysia*, 8 IJPHCS 87, 95 (2021).

alive.[84] Islamic scholars have diverging opinions on whether artificial respiration would amount to actual breathing.[85] No law exists in Pakistan that mentions anything about brain death.[86] Significant confusion regarding acceptance of brain death exists in the Middle East. Conflicting opinions among the Islamic scholars have shaped the public resentment against brain death in Saudi Arabia and Egypt.[87]

Oman has clear-cut criteria and protocols to diagnose brain death but lacks uniform guidelines across the country.[88] Law in Qatar permits the use of the neurological criteria to determine death in the context of organ transplants, however, there is widespread distrust among the public regarding the concept.[89] Misconceptions surrounding brain death and conservative religious beliefs stop families from consenting to the determination of brain death in Iran[90] and Jordan.[91]

---

[84] Machado C., Kerein J., et al., *The Concept of Brain Death did not Evolve to Benefit Organ Transplants*, 33 J Med. Ethics 197, 197-200 (2007).

[85] Bedir A., Aksoy S., *Brain Death Revisited: It is not 'Complete Death' according to Islamic Sources*, 37 J. Med. Ethics 290, 294 (2011).

[86] Mughis Sheerani, Mian Urfy et. al., *Brain Death: Concepts and Knowledge amongst Health Professionals in Province of Sindh, Pakistan*, 58 JPMA 352, 354-355 (2008).

[87] Abdul Al-Hashim, Mujahid Al-Busaidi, *Understanding the Concept of Brain Death in the Middle East*, 30 OMJ 75, 75-76 (2015).

[88] *Id.*

[89] George S., Thomas M., et al., *Somatic Survival and Organ Donation among Brain-dead patients in the State of Qatar*, 16 Neurol., 207, 207-208 (2016).

[90] Abbasi P., Nouri P., et al., *The Obstacles to Organ Donation Following Brain Death in Iran: A Qualitative Study*, 21 BMC Med. Ethics 83, 83 (2020).

[91] Hammad S., Fawzi M., et al., *Questionnaire on Brain Death and Organ Procurement*, 15 Exp. Clin Transplant 121, 121-123 (2017).

Israel occupies a peculiar position in the map of countries that have accepted brain death in Asia. Orthodox Jews do not recognize brain death as death.[92] The traditional rabbinic approaches to determine death can be divided into two sects. One sect that believes that cessation of all bodily functions leads to death, and the other sect that believes death occurs when breathing stops.[93] In the 20th century, some Jewish scholars came up with the proposal that there could be a third criterion to determine death, which involves the loss of neurological function.[94] Several Rabbis published articles supporting the notion that Halakhic death equates to brain death.[95]

In 1986, the Chief Rabbinate of the country ruled in favor of brain-stem death and identified it to be a criterion to determine death in the context of organ transplants.[96] However, the same was not well-received by most of the orthodox Jews. The Brain-Respiratory Death Act was enacted in Israel to support organ procurement, which provided for religious exceptions to the determination of

---

[92] Inwald D, Jakobovits I, Petros A., Brain Stem Death: *Managing Care When Accepted Medical Guidelines and Religious Beliefs are in Conflict: Consideration and Compromise are Possible*, 320 BMJ 1266, 1266-1267 (2000).

[93] Rabbi Jason Weiner, *Death v. Brain Death in Judaism*, MY JEWISH LEARNING (Jan. 2, 2023, 6:56 AM), https://www.myjewishlearning.com/article/defining-death-in-jewish-law/

[94] *Id.*

[95] Rabbi Moshe D. Tendler, *Halakhic Death Means Brain Death*, 3 The Jew. Rev. 5750, 5751 (1990).

[96] NAFTALI MOSES, REALLY DEAD? THE ISRAELI BRAIN-DEATH CONTROVERSY 1967-1986 (1st ed. 2011).

brain death and apnea test.[97] The law intended to give reasonable, religious accommodations. But the resentment against the concept of brain death in the orthodox Jewish circles rendered it unsuccessful.

The view that brain death is death has been accepted by Reform, Conservative, and some Modern Orthodox Jews.[98] The Rabbinical Council of America affirmed through a 110-page report that brain-stem death is an acceptable criterion to determine death.[99] However, the study report was not a formal ruling. This again sparked heated debates among Jews on whether to accept brain death or not. There is no uniform acceptance of the concept of brain death among the Jewish community.

---

[97] Gabbay E., Fins J., *Go in Peace: Brain Death, Reasonable Accommodation and Jewish Mourning Rituals*, 58 J. Relig. Health 1672, 1679 (2019).

[98] *See supra note* 93.

[99] RABBINICAL COUNCIL OF AMERICA, HALACHIC ISSUES IN THE DETERMINATION OF DEATH AND IN ORGAN TRANSPLANTATION (2010).

CHAPTER

03

OUTLINING THE LEGAL HISTORY OF BRAIN DEATH: THE JOURNEY TO THE UDDA IN THE UNITED STATES

The innovations in emergency medicine and the introduction of artificial life support devices questioned the traditional approach to the determination of death. This prompted the medical profession to reconsider the age-old definition of death. Neurological criteria began to be considered yet another yardstick to determine death, apart from cardiopulmonary criteria. Interestingly, the medical profession started to view death as a process.[100] However, as discussed earlier, law needed to ascertain death as a momentary event to avoid complications. A uniform standard to determine death could impact the outcomes of several legal quandaries related to medical malpractice[101], criminal liability[102], and family inheritance.[103] Although solid organ failure rattled the medical

[100] H.L. Hirsh, *Brain Death*, 21 MED. TRIAL TECH Q. 377, 378-379 (1975) (concluding that human beings die in stages, proceeding through clinical death to brain death, to biological death, and ultimately cellular death).
[101] Tucker v. Lower, 1 Va. Cir. 124 (1972).
[102] Commonwealth v. Golston, 366 N.E.2d 744 (1977).
[103] Schmitt v. Pierce, 344 S.W.2d 120 (1961).

professionals across the world since the early 1900s, cutting-edge technology in organ transplants that emerged during the latter half of the 20th century shed light on the possibility to prolong life of a terminally ill patient.[104] So, in order to foster organ donations and transplants without having to fear legal obstacles, a uniform standard of death was required in the United States that would include the latest concept of brain death.

In the 1960s, the National Conference of Commissioners on Uniform State Laws (NCCUSL) held thorough deliberations to formulate a legal metric to encourage organ donation and related research. As a culmination of their efforts, the Uniform Anatomical Gift Act (UAGA) came into being in 1968. The statute had a noble objective; but it did not mention anything about the standards to determine the death of potential organ donors. It is pertinent to note that the common law standard of determining death that predominantly existed during this time period was the cardiopulmonary criterion. This impacted the effectiveness of UAGA, as there were states that still relied on the traditional standard.

At the same time, some courts observed that the organ donations from brain dead patients were more viable for transplantation as compared to other donors.[105] This meant that the organ retrieval

---

[104] Anamika Krishnan, *UDBHR: An Interpretation in the Indian Medico-Legal and Bioethical Context*, 214, 227 in BIOETHICS OF THE CRAZY APE (Oguz Kelemen, Gergely Tari ed., 2019).

[105] New York City Health & Hosp. Corp. v. Sulsona, 367 N.Y.S.2d 686, 689-90 (1975) (expert testimony signified that the kidneys obtained from

and transplants in states following the traditional standard were most often prone to failure. Even when some courts in such states assented to the application of brain death criteria[106], physicians were afraid to proceed with it as they anticipated criminal liability.[107] A physician in a common law jurisdiction could be held liable for homicide if she withdrew life support from a patient who exhibited cardiopulmonary functions.[108]

In the attempt to unify the standards of determining death, Kansas became the first state to enact a law referring to brain death in 1970.[109] The statute provides alternative criteria for determining death, rather than unifying them. So, a physician could either choose between the cardiopulmonary criteria or neurological criteria to determine death. This circulated the wrong idea among the common masses that cardiopulmonary death and brain death are different phenomena, and there could be two types of death.[110] In 1975, the American Bar Association (ABA) published a Model Definition of Death Act, which did

---

donors pronounced dead through the cardiopulmonary criteria were more prone to post-operative failure).

[106] *Id.*

[107] Guthrie, *Brain Death and Criminal Liability*, 15 CRIM. L. BULL. 40, 42 (1979).

[108] Eichner v. Dillon, 52 N.Y.S.2d 517, 533 (1980).

[109] Burkle C.M., Sharp R.R., et al., *Why Brain Death is Considered Death and Why There Should be No Confusion*, 83 Neurol., 1464, 1469 (2014).

[110] Alexander Capron, Leon Kass, *A Statutory Definition of the Standards for Determining Human Death: An Appraisal and a Proposal*, 121 U. PENN. L. REV. 87 (1972) (they drafted a model law wherein death could be assessed using the brain death criteria only under circumstances where artificial means of support preclude a determination that spontaneous

not have any provision that expressly endorsed both standards of determination of death.

The NCCUSL approved a Uniform Brain Death Act in 1978, that adopted the concept of brain death as death for all legal and medical purposes. The American Medical Association (AMA) had always remained skeptical about legalizing the brain death standard. The entity feared that enacting a law to codify the same would prove to be too rigid to accept future scientific innovations. But later, they realized that they could support a model law, which would not identify "specific" neurological criteria.[111] In 1978, the AMA drafted and published a Model Determination of Death Act[112]. Hence, by 1979, various independent model statutes were adopted in the country. Even though there were differences in how each of these organizations approached the brain death standard, they had a consensus on the dire need to adopt a uniform standard to determine death. The representatives of these three organizations ratified the new Act in 1981[113], which came to be called as the Uniform Determination of Death Act (hereinafter referred to as UDDA).

---

and respiratory and circulatory functions have ceased; but this model law was also ambiguous).

[111] Veith, Fein, Tendler, et al., *Brain Death – Part II: A Status Report of Legal Considerations*, 238 JAMA, 1744, 1745 (1977).

[112] *AMA Insights*, 243 JAMA, 419, 420 (1980).

[113] *A.B.A: The Voice of the Profession – Annual Report 1980-81*, 67 A.B.A.J. 1479 (1981) (explaining the intent of UDDA to reduce uncertainty in this crucial medical-legal arena).

The UDDA aims to provide a broad, legally and medically sound foundation to determine death.[114] However, the scope of the model law is limited as it neither defines death or the right to die with dignity.[115] There are only three provisions under the model law and they talk about the determination of death[116], uniformity of construction and application[117], and the short title.[118] It does not set forth the standard medical procedures and tests to be carried out to determine death. This gap should have been intentional as technological advancements would render any strict set of medical standards obsolete every few years. Thus, courts are vested with the power to recognize contemporary, accepted standards of medical practice. UDDA defines brain death as the full and irreversible loss of all functioning throughout the whole brain, including the brain stem, in conformity with recognized medical standards.[119] All the states in the country have adopted the whole-brain death criteria.[120] As of 2023, 43 states have adopted the UDDA.[121]

---

[114] *See supra note* 33.

[115] *Id.*

[116] *Id.* § 1

[117] *Id.* § 2.

[118] *Id.* § 3.

[119] *Guidelines for the determination of death. Report of the medical consultants on the diagnosis of death to the President's Commission for the Study of Ethical Problems in Medicine and Biomedical and Behavioral Research*, 246 JAMA 2184-6 (1981).

[120] *See supra note* 109.

[121] DETERMINATION OF DEATH ACT, https://www.uniformlaws.org/committees/community-home?CommunityKey=155faf5d-03c2-4027-99ba-ee4c99019d6c (last visited Jan. 27, 2023).

CHAPTER

04

THE LAW OF BRAIN DEATH IN INDIA

India is the world's most populous democracy[122] and the seventh largest country by area.[123] It has the longest written constitution,[124] which is quasi-federal in nature.[125] There is a unique blend of unitary and federal features that widen the scope for national integration, co-operation, single market economy, and resolution of inter-state conflicts. The Indian Polity is not federal where distinct, individual states could have joined to form a union as in the United States of America.[126] The Indian Parliament is vested with enormous powers to form a state, alter its boundary, or even change its name.[127] The Indian Constitution is a combination of federal and unitary elements, inclining more towards the latter.[128] The government structure has two tiers,

[122] Kartikeyan Sundaram, *India's Population Has Already Overtaken China's, Analysts Estimate*, BLOOMBERG (Jan. 17, 2023, 11:49 PM), https://www.bloomberg.com/news/articles/2023-01-18/india-s-population-overtakes-china-to-become-world-s-biggest-analysts-estimate?leadSource=uverify%20wall.

[123] UNITED NATIONS STATISTICS DIVISION, https://unstats.un.org/UNSDWebsite/ (last visited Jan. 18, 2023).

[124] M.V. PYLEE, INDIA'S CONSTITUTION 3, (5th ed. 1994).

[125] THE CONSTITUTION OF INDIA, 1950, Part XI.

[126] State of Karnataka v. Union of India & Anr. (1978) 2 SCR 1. (Ind.).

[127] S.R. Bommai & Ors. v. Union of India & Ors. (1994) 3 SCC 1. (Ind.).

[128] *Id.*

along with provisions for local governance.[129] India is a sovereign, secular, democratic, republic.[130]

"Decolonizing Bioethics" ~ Illustration Courtesy:
Aswath C. (India)

[129] *See supra note* 125, Art.1.
[130] *Id.*, Preamble.

Colonialism and its Aftermath: An Indian Narrative

"If you do not condemn colonialism,

If you do not side with colonial people,

What kind of revolution are you waging?"[131]

Prior to the British arrival, India's education system remained fragmented, however the institutions imparted knowledge in languages, grammar, theology, logic, law, mathematics, metaphysics, and medicine.[132] The Indian subcontinent had various systems of medicine and healing dating back to 4500 B.C. India developed a comprehensive form of healing called Ayurveda that relied on the medicinal values of herbs, which is now considered as a Complementary Alternative Medicine (CAM). Ayurvedahadvarioussubsetsthatdealtwithsurgery, general medicine, gynecology, and psychiatry. It emerged as a completely advanced analytical theory of health and disease.[133] It grew through rigorous discourses and discussions.[134] Medical education

[131] Ho Chi Minh, *The Path that Led Me to Leninism*, in DECOLONIZATION 47-49 (Raymond F. Betts ed., 2004).
[132] A COMPREHENSIVE HISTORY OF INDIA – PART 3 (P.N. Chopra & M.N. Das et. al. eds., 2003).
[133] Anu Saini, *Physicians of Ancient India* 5 J Family Med. Prim. Care 254, 255-256 (2016).
[134] Y.N. Nuraliev, *Doctor's Ethics in Ancient East Written Classics and in the Works of Middle Age Medical Scientists* in 2 INTERACTIONS BETWEEN INDIAN AND CENTRAL ASIAN SCIENCE AND TECHNOLOGY IN MEDIEVAL TIMES 11-8 (W.H. Abdi, M.S. Asimov, et.al. eds., 1990).

was intensive, and the training was imparted by the teachers in their small institutions called *Ashrams*.[135] Training focused not only on medicinal knowledge and healing but also on character-building, memory power, academic performance, and honesty[136] of the medical students.[137]

Ayurveda had elaborate procedures about how to diagnose death, which were summarized in ancient scriptures, namely, *Charaka Samhita, Astangahrudayam,* and *Sushruta Samhita.*[138] One school of thought opined that if there is a bluish discoloration of the lips, rigor mortis, absence of cold shivers or goose bumps even after smearing cold water, the patient should be considered dead as further treatment would be futile.[139] Another text on surgery held that if blood does not flow after an incision and if the tongue turns white and lower jaw is unstable, further treatment would be futile.[140] Both of these schools of thought date back to 600 BC. Around 200 BC, scholars shifted focus onto a close observation of breathing, loss of control over senses, and pupil movements. The later scriptures reveal these changes. If a person does not regain

---

[135] *Id.*

[136] *See supra note* 133.

[137] K. LOCHAN, MEDICINES OF EARLY INDIA 90 (1st ed. 2003).

[138] Gopendra C. Kamal, Sourav Ballav et. al., *Evolution of Diagnostic Techniques of Death: Ayurveda Perspective and Modern Trends in India*, 6 IJRG 109, 110 (2018).

[139] CHARAKA SAMHITA (V.J. Trikamji ed. 2014) (this is considered to be the most authentic reference to Ayurveda).

[140] SUSHRUTA SAMHITA (V.J. Trikamji ed. 2014) (originally written by Sushruta, who is considered to be the father of Surgery).

consciousness by nasal medication[141], does not respond to cold water being sprinkled over the body and ears[142], and if there is no movement of eyeballs, these were regarded as the signs to confirm death. Hence, the primary criteria of declaring death revolved around brain, heart, and lungs.[143]

The British Empire rejected the faith-based education system and supplanted it with structures with a colonial design.[144] The new system fostered mere memorization[145] of the newly introduced English language rather than an intellectual inquiry into the concepts taught. This education system gave rise to a class distinction and spawned animosity between the class that received English education and the class that was deprived of this opportunity, which in turn aided the British motive of divide and rule.[146]

At the same time, it is true that various scientific advancements emanated from colonialism. But these achievements in turn became the tools of the empire

---

141 C.K. NAMBOODIRI, VISHAVAIDYASARAMUCHAYA (1st ed. 2006) (this is a treatise on toxicology with special reference to the physicians in the State of Kerala).

142 K. MAHADEVASASTRIKAL, VISHA VAIDYA JYOTSNIKA: AN ENGLISH TRANSLATION (3rd ed. 1958).

143 *See supra note* 138, 116.

144 Aziz Rahman, Mohsin Ali, et. al., *The British Art of Colonialism in India: Subjugation and Division*, 25 J. Peace Confl. Stud. 2, 7-8 (2018) (discussing the introduction of a British-styled curriculum in India and its failure).

145 C. Whitehead, *The Historiography of British Education Policy, Part 1: India*, 34 Hist. Educ. 300, 315-329 (2005).

146 *See supra note* 144, 9.

to control the colonies.[147][148] A closer examination of history will show that advancements in the treatment of tropical diseases were made not out of any consideration for the people who were subject to colonial control, but rather to keep colonial agents and soldiers healthy.[149] This also meant the extinction of indigenous science. The endeavors to control the outbreak of communicable diseases gave the empire unlimited power to control the people in the colonies and spread the notion that indigenous science is superfluous and ineffective.[150]

India became independent on August 15, 1947. The Constitution laid bricks of foundational changes in the legal framework of healthcare in the country. It demarcates the lawmaking powers distributed between the Union Government and the State Governments.[151] The Seventh Schedule contains three distinct lists – Union, State, and Concurrent lists.[152] The Union list contains subjects on which the Parliament of India can make laws for the entire nation. The State list enumerates

---

[147] D. ARNOLD, SCIENCE, TECHNOLOGY AND MEDICINE IN COLONIAL INDIA (1st ed. 2000).

[148] D. ARNOLD, COLONIZING THE BODY: STATE MEDICINE AND EPIDEMIC DISEASE IN NINETEENTH CENTURY INDIA (1st ed. 1993).

[149] R.D. Roy, *The Untold Story of Modern Science is One of Empire and Colonial Exploitation*, QUARTZ (Apr. 9, 2018, 6:56 AM), https://qz.com/india/1247577/the-untold-story-of-modern-science-is-one-of-empire-and-colonial-exploitation.

[150] M.A. Alam, *Imperialism and Science*, 4 Soc. Scien. 3, 6-15 (1977) (discussing the attempts to smother local scientific knowledge).

[151] *See supra note* 125, Art. 246.

[152] *Id.*

the subjects on which the state legislatures have power to regulate. The concurrent list is unique as it contains subjects on which both the Parliament and state legislatures have jurisdiction. Public health, hospitals, and dispensaries fall under the state list. Regulation of medical profession falls within the concurrent list. This places healthcare in a peculiar position wherein both Union and State governments may intervene independently and jointly. In addition to the lawmaking powers granted to the government(s), the judiciary has proactively interpreted the constitutional right to life to include the right to healthcare.[153] This is the foundation of universal healthcare in India. With respect to alternate systems of medicine, the Government of India has established a separate ministry called AYUSH (Ayurveda, Yoga Medicine, Unani, Siddha, Homeopathy) to foster research and development in traditional medicine and indigenous science.

Law, Death, and Brainstem Death

There is no uniform definition of death in India. However, two statutes have attempted to define death in their own specific contexts. Section 46 of the Indian Penal Code[154] defines death as the death of a human being unless the context indicates otherwise. This definition is made in the context of criminal

[153] Bandhua Mukti Morcha v. Union of India & Ors. (1997) 10 SCC 549; State of Punjab & Ors. v. Mohinder Singh Chawla, AIR 1997 SC 1225 (Ind.).

[154] Act No. 45/1860 (Ind.).

law. According to section 2(1)(b) of the Registration of Births and Deaths Act[155] a person dies when all the signs of life permanently disappear at any point following live birth. This definition is made in the context of the collection of information regarding births and deaths for statistical purposes of the government.

It was in 1994 that the Union Government enacted the Transplantation of Human Organs and Tissues Act[156] (hereinafter referred to as THOTA), that defined death and brain-stem death for the first time. Death is defined as the complete loss of all signs of life due to brainstem death or cardiopulmonary collapse at any point following live birth.[157] Brain-stem death has been defined as the stage at which all functions of the brainstem have permanently and irreversibly ceased.[158]

It is interesting to observe that India follows the U.K. model in defining death. This fact highlights the dire need to distinguish 'whole brain' and 'brainstem' criteria in determining a person's death. Whole brain concept relies on the fact that an individual who has lost all the functions of her brain, including the brainstem is considered to be dead. This formulation is reflected in UDDA, and major laws related defining death by neurological criteria in European countries. However, in U.K.

---

[155] Act No. 18/1969 (Ind.).
[156] Act No. 42/1994 (Ind.).
[157] *Id.* Section 2(e).
[158] *Id.* Section 2(d).

and India, the medical community and lawmakers have intentionally adopted brainstem death as the yardstick to determine one's death. The laws in these countries do not require all functions of the brain to end, rather requires that none of the functions, even if present, must indicate consciousness.[159] The focus here is on consciousness and respiratory control.[160] The clinical determination for both criteria remains the same, albeit the confirmatory tests vary. Brainstem approach comparatively places a diminished burden of proof.[161] At the same time, whole brain death is relatively an approximation as some neuroendocrine responses remain even after clinical determination of brain death.[162]

In India, two formats of death certificate are available – one under the Registration of Births and Deaths Act signifying the death of a person, and another under the Transplantation of Human Organs Rules of 1995[163] indicating brainstem death.

---

[159] Peter Simpson, David Bates et. al., *A Code of Practice for the Diagnosis and Confirmation of Death: 2008*, AMRC, https://www.aomrc.org.uk/reports-guidance/ukdec-reports-and-guidance/code-practice-diagnosis-confirmation-death/.

[160] *Diagnosis of Brain Death: Statement issued by the Honorary Secretary of the Conference of Medical Royal Colleges and their Faculties in the United Kingdom on 11 October 1976*, 2 Br. Med J. 1187, 1187-1188 (1976).

[161] Baron L., Shemie S.D., et al., *Brief Review: History, Concept and Controversies in the Neurological Determination of Death*, 53 Can J Anaesth., 602, 602-608 (2006).

[162] Smith M., *Brain Death: Time for an International Consensus*, 108 BJA i6, i7 (2012).

[163] THE GAZETTE OF INDIA: EXTRAORDINARY (1995), https://notto.gov.in/WriteReadData/Portal/images/THOA-Rules-2014.pdf (Forms 8 and 10).

They are not identical. Only the former certificate serves as an admissible piece of evidence for most of the administrative procedure and litigation. The latter certificate cannot be even used as a proof for presenting an insurance claim.[164] This means that since brain death has not been statutorily declared as death, a certificate declaring brain death may not be accepted as a proof of death for legal purposes. The problem lies in the fact that THOTA is only invoked in the light of organ transplantation. Unless the patient's organs or tissues are to be donated, doctors do not have the statutory duty to determine brainstem death or even perform confirmatory tests on a possibly brain-dead patient.[165] Thus, brain death remains a taboo in the country. There is a widespread distrust in the healthcare system with respect to brain death as people are generally afraid that physicians declare brain death only for illegally harvesting the organs of the patient.

Critical Analysis of THOTA

Organ donation rate in India is merely 0.6 per million, pushing the country into a vicious crisis.[166] Last year, an expert team at the University of

---

[164] Sonali Vadi, Sunil Shroff, *Redefining Death: Urgent Need to Evolve Toward a Homogenous Definition of Death in India*, 10 IJCCC 368, 368-369 (2019).

[165] *Id.*

[166] Milan Sharma, Gulam Jeelani, *India's Organ Crisis Deepens*, INDIA TODAY (Jan. 05, 2020, 02:29 AM), https://www.indiatoday.in/mail-today/story/india-s-organ-crisis-deepens-1634029-2020-01-04.

Bedfordshire conducted the first ever review[167] of barriers to deceased organ donation among Indians across the world. The study found that knowledge of brain death was rare among the participants.[168][169] Family opposition[170][171], religious objections[172], and disinterest[173] proved to be the factors why participants were reluctant to register as organ donors. Fear about misuse of organs by healthcare institutions was another factor contributing to the organ crisis.[174] Instead of eradicating these barriers, THOTA indirectly keeps them in place.

THOTA has created an illusion amongst the medical community that they should declare death

[167] Britzer P. Vincent, Gurch Randhawa et al., *Barriers Towards Deceased Organ Donation among Indians Living Globally: An Integrative Systematic Review Using Narrative Synthesis*, 12 BMJ 1-18 (2022).

[168] Poreddi V., Sunitha T.S., et al., *Gender Differences in Perceptions and Attitudes of General Population Towards Organ Donation: An Indian Perspective*, 28 Saudi J. Kidney Dis Transpl. 599 (2017).

[169] Bharambe V.K. HR M., et al, *Awareness Regarding Body and Organ Donation Amongst the Population of an Urban City in India*, 5 J Health allied Sci NU 51, 51-57 (2015).

[170] Balajee K.L., Ramachandran N., et al., *Awareness and Attitudes Toward Organ Donation in Rural Puducherry, India*, 6 Ann Med Health Sci Res 286, 287-289 (2016).

[171] Basavarajegowda A., Arjunan C., et al., *A Comparative Study of Knowledge, Attitude, and Practices About Organ Donation Among Blood Donors and Non-Blood Donors*, 15 Asian J Transfus Sci 56 (2021).

[172] Wong L.P., *Factors Limiting Deceased Organ Donation: Focus Groups' Perspective from Culturally Diverse Community*, 42 Transplant Proc 1439, 1439-1444 (2010).

[173] Joshi M.S., *Whose Decision Is It? Organ Donation Attitudes Among Young UK South Asians*, 56 Psychol Stud, 86, 86-97 (2011).

[174] Mishra P.R., Mohakud S., et al., *A Comparison Between Medical and Non-Medical Students in India for Cadaveric Organ Donation*, 33 J Fore Med Toxicol 5, 5-12 (2016).

using the brainstem death criteria only if organ donation is in question.[175] Let us take a look at some hypothetical scenarios. A patient is brought into the intensive care unit of a hospital, and her chances of survival are extremely low. The attending physician has a duty to inquire if the patient has authorized to donate her organs or tissues after death.[176] If the patient has consented already or consents upon inquiry, the medical team proceeds to certify brainstem death.[177] Now, another patient who was brought into the hospital dies. The attending physician has a duty to ask the deceased patient's family or friends whether she had authorized organ donation before death. If she had consented to organ donation prior to death, and the near relatives do not object to the donation procedure[178], then the medical team goes ahead to certify brainstem death.

The key issue to be noted here is that family consent is mandated for organ donation, even if the person had consented to it before her death. Scholars have argued that family consent is beneficial in organ transplant statutes as it minimizes the distress of the family members, builds trust among the people regarding organ donation process, and

[175] Noble Gracious, Veena Roshan Jose, *Certification of Brain Stem Death in India: Medico-Legal Perspectives*, 16 Amrita J Med, 71, 71-76 (2020).
[176] *See supra note* 156, § 3(1A) (i).
[177] *Id.* § 3(5).
[178] *Id.* § 3(3).

solely depending on the wishes of the deceased may be problematic.[179]

But, alternately, not respecting a mentally competent adult's wishes have disastrous consequences. It is a blatant violation of personal autonomy, which is a person's rational capability for self-determination.[180] Right to bodily autonomy has been identified as a subset of the constitutional right to life and personal liberty.[181] It is not uncommon for family members to challenge organ donation. However, when a statute paves the way to allow such a violation of privacy and bodily autonomy, it is unethical and unconstitutional. The autonomy discussed here is not that of the deceased, but of a living person who made a choice about her body after death.[182] In a nutshell, brainstem death is not generally determined unless organ donation is in the picture.

The legislature must harmonize the different legal definitions of death. A person may be dead under THOTA but may be alive under the Registration of Births and Deaths Act because in the event of brain death, there may still be biological signs of life, and

[179] David Shaw, Dale Gardiner, et al., *Family over Rules? An Ethical Analysis of Allowing Families to Overrule Donation Intentions*, 101 Transplant. 482, 482-487 (2017).

[180] VAUGHN L., BIOETHICS: PRINCIPLES, ISSUES AND CASES (1st ed. 2016).

[181] Navtej Singh Johar v. Union of India, AIR 2018 SC 4321 (Ind.).

[182] A. Sharif, Moorlock G., *Influencing Relatives to Respect Donor Autonomy: Should We Nudge Families to Consent to Organ Donation?*, 32 Bioethics 155, 156-163 (2017).

there is no permanent disappearance of all evidence of life. While THOTA authorizes organ retrieval from brain dead persons, it may be an offence under the Indian Penal Code. There are no uniform guidelines regarding the process of determination of brainstem death in the country. It is up to the surrogates to determine how long a person on ventilator needs to be on such life-support.

Standard Operating Procedure in Kerala: Lessons for the Union Government

Kerala is a state in southern India, and has the highest literacy rate, the highest Human Development Index (HDI)[183], the highest life expectancy, the highest sex ratio, and the eighth largest economy in the country. The Kerala Model of Development is a well-known economic model with HDI indicators better than many developed countries, high levels of political participation, health-focused public policies, and poverty eradication programs.[184] The Kerala model of public health received international acclaim for how it handled the unprecedented waves of the COVID-19 pandemic, when the rest of the country experienced chaos and steeping number of deaths.[185]

---

[183] Press Trust of India, *At 96.2% Kerala Tops India's Literacy Rate Chart Again*, FIRSTPOST (Sep. 08, 2020, 13:37 PM), https://www.firstpost.com/india/at-96-2-kerala-tops-indias-literacy-rate-chart-again-andhra-pradesh-ranks-lowest-with-66-4-8796401.html

[184] GOVINDA PARAYIL, KERALA: THE DEVELOPMENT EXPERIENCE (1st ed. 2000).

[185] Jos Chathukulam, Joseph Tharamangalam, *The Kerala Model in the Time of COVID-19: Rethinking State, Society and Democracy*, 137 World

In early 2017, a Public Interest Litigation[186] (equivalent to social action litigation in the U.S.) was filed by one Dr. S. Ganapathy to bring attention to the alleged malpractice of utilizing the brainstem death declaration to illegally harvest organs in the hospitals in Kerala. He alleged that EEG was not used, and instead, apnea testing was improperly done to camouflage the actual state of affairs to the family or friends of the patient. The medical ignorance of the patient(s) and family are preyed upon to facilitate organ trafficking. While disposing the writ petition, the High Court of Kerala emphasized on the need to streamline the process to declare brainstem death and directed the State of Kerala to issue a uniform protocol to address the issue.[187] In response to the order of the court, the state government issued the Standard Operating Procedure (hereinafter called as the SOP) for Brain Death Certification in Government and Private Hospitals in the State of Kerala on 3rd April 2018.[188]

The SOP sets forth a detailed procedure to determine brainstem death. The brain stem death certification panel or committee shall consist of four doctors, a registered medical practitioner who

---

Dev. 105207 (2021).

[186] Dr. S. Ganapathy v. State of Kerala, WP(C) No. 5552 of 2017, High Court of Kerala. (Ind.)

[187] *Id.* 3.

[188] HEALTH AND FAMILY WELFARE DEPARTMENT, GOVERNMENT OF KERALA, STANDARD OPERATING PROCEDURE FOR BRAIN DEATH CERTIFICATION IN GOVERNMENT AND PRIVATE HOSPITALS IN THE STATE (2018) https://www.knos.org.in/pdf/53-2018-BRAIN%20DEATH-SOP.pdf.

serves as the hospital's in-charge, a registered and qualified medical practitioner designated by the appropriate authority (from a panel formed by the government), a neurologist or neurosurgeon, and a registered medical practitioner who has been treating the patient.[189] Prior to determining the irreversible and proximate cause of coma, the committee should rule out any reversible causes of coma.[190] Thereafter, two series of test must be performed in the presence of all the members of the certification panel at an interval of 6 hours to assess the absence of brain stem functions.[191] If these tests do not confirm the presence of brain stem reflexes, an apnea test should be performed after obtaining informed written consent from the surrogate decision maker. If clinical findings are unreliable, the physicians have the option not to proceed with the declaration of brain stem death.[192] Improvement in hypotension, metabolic acidosis and pre-oxygenation is mandatory prior to the apnea test. If the panel feels that residual neuromuscular blockade should be tested, they may do so by adhering to the protocol.[193]

However, the SOP has still room for improvement. The SOP only discusses brain stem death declaration in the context of organ transplantation. The order does not attempt to separate the concept of brain

---

[189] *Id.*

[190] *Id.* 1.

[191] *Id.* 2,3.

[192] *Id.* 4.

[193] *Id.*

stem death from organ retrieval. It mentions that in the case of unavailability of a neurologist or neurosurgeon, any physician and anesthetist can replace her on the medical committee. This points towards the question whether they have the adequate knowledge and training in neuroscience to bring in the perspective of a neurologist.

Nonetheless, the SOP provides critical lessons for the Union Government of India. The SOP embodies the four core principles of bioethics. Since the SOP highlights the importance of getting written consent from the surrogate decision maker before the apnea test, it recognizes the autonomy of the patient and her family members or friends. The SOP strives to ensure accuracy in the determination of brain death that seeks to improve the quality of care and informed decision-making, thus embodying the principle of beneficence. The detailed guidelines on performing all possible core and ancillary tests to determine brain death ensure non-maleficence. Only a government-appointed medical committee can certify brain death. This is aimed at ensuring fairness and equity. Thus, these guidelines are at par with the ethical guidelines issued by most of the developed nations. Now that we have an excellent model of guidelines, we need a homogenous definition of death.

Illustration Courtesy: *Aswath C. (India)*

CHAPTER

05

DETERMINING BRAIN DEATH AS DEATH: THE ETHICAL INQUIRY AND THE EVALUATION OF ARGUMENTS

Since this work is a law and ethics paper, it is inevitable to discuss the key bioethical theories that create a comprehensive framework to analyze the ethical implications of brain death. The three main key theories being discussed in this section are deontology, utilitarianism, and virtue ethics. Deontology focus on the ethics of duty that is performed by an individual.[194] The nature of action is given due consideration in such a manner that no harm is allowed.[195] This theory focuses on the inherent value of human life, emphasizing the four bioethical principles.[196] The intention of the action is more important than the consequences.[197] On the other hand, utilitarianism focuses on the maximization of positive outcomes.[198] The

---

[194] *See supra note* 11.
[195] *Id.*
[196] Donaldson T.M., *Ethical Resources for the Clinician: Principles, Values and Other Theories*, in CONTEMPORARY ISSUES IN BIOETHICS 15-38 (Beauchamp ed., 2003).
[197] IMMANUEL KANT, CRITIQUE OF JUDGMENT (1st ed. 1987).
[198] JEREMY BENTHAM, AN INTRODUCTION TO THE PRINCIPLES OF MORALS AND LEGISLATION (1st ed. 1823).

usefulness of the action is given importance over the nature of the action.[199] Virtue ethics is entirely different from these theories because it focuses on the individual's character and virtues to assess the righteousness of her actions.[200] It analyzes candor, equity, and civility to decide whether the action was right or wrong.[201] Thus, deontology concentrates on the duty, utilitarianism focuses on the consequences of the action, and virtue ethics explores the character of the individual who acts.[202]

Deontology and virtue ethics revolve around the moral importance of the actors, and utilitarianism concerns itself with the nature of consequences. These three theories are applied in medical ethics to create a framework for ethical analysis, guide the moral behavior of individuals in healthcare settings, and address the ethical dilemmas in clinical decision-making.[203] Deontology requires the healthcare professionals to do no harm, and respect the patient's autonomy and confidentiality.[204]

---

[199] *Id.*

[200] Alexandra S., *Virtue Ethics and Its Potential as the Leading Moral Theory*, 12 Discussions 1, 1-2 (2015).

[201] Zuckerman S., Gerrit K., et al., *Surprising Pandemic Experiences: A Confrontation Between Principle-Based and Virtue Ethics, and A Plea for Virtue Ethics Training for Medical Students and Residents*, 1 J. Eval Clin Pract. 1, 1-8 (2023).

[202] Vincent Triola, *Differences Between Virtue, Utilitarianism and Deontological Ethics*, VINCENT TRIOLA (Mar. 25, 2021), https://vincenttriola.com/blogs/ten-years-of-academic-writing/what-are-the-differences-between-virtue-utilitarianism-deontological-ethics.

[203] Basil Varkey, *Principles of Clinical Ethics and Their Application to Practice*, 30 Med Princ Pract 17, 17-28 (2021).

[204] *Id.*

Utilitarianism guides them to place importance on the well-being and safety of the patients.[205] Virtue ethics emphasizes on the need for healthcare professionals to be trustworthy and empathetic.[206]

In brain death determination, deontological ethics guide the healthcare professionals to do the right thing. It requires them to respect a patient's autonomy and her decision to continue or withdraw the life-sustaining treatment. The duty to do no harm ensures that no medical intervention is made without the consent of the patient or her surrogate decision maker. However, the lack of consistency of the brain death determination criteria makes it difficult to apply deontological ethics in a meaningful way. Utilitarian perspective would be to recognize brain death as death because it opens up the possibility of organ transplants to save numerous lives. It ensures optimum allocation of resources. However, this approach may focus on the cost-effectiveness of the procedures instead of human dignity. Virtue ethics require the healthcare professionals to deal with the patient and her surrogate decision maker or family with empathy and sensitivity. It mandates that the healthcare professionals should engage in an open and honest conversation with the patient and her family. But virtue ethics can often be highly subjective as the good or bad traits in a human being shall depend on the independent moral values of the individual.

---

[205] *Id.*

[206] *Id.*

The procedure and parameters of determining death have evolved over the past few centuries. Likewise, the definitions of death have also changed. As of 2023, we have scientists discussing the possibility of introducing a neurorespiratory criteria to determine death.[207] The basic assumptions made in the definitions of death are loss of vital organ functions, irreversibility of such loss, lack of consciousness, and absence of responses to the apnea and related ancillary tests. Despite the widespread consensus within the international medical community, there are several arguments against determining brain death as biological death or Death by Neurologic Criteria (hereinafter referred to as DNC). This section attempts to break down each of those arguments, analyze the sub-arguments, and rebut them.

Argument 1: Brain death is not biological death.

Several philosophers argue that brain death is not actual death.[208][209][210] Many philosophers call it

---

[207] Greer, D.M., Shemie S.D., et al., *Determination of Brain Death/Death by Neurologic Criteria: The World Brain Death Project*, 324 JAMA 1078, 1081 (2010).

[208] Verheijde, L. Joseph, Rady, Y. Mohamed, et al., *Neuroscience and Brain Death Controversies: The Elephant in the Room*, 57 J. Relig. Health 1745, 1746 (2018).

[209] Nair-Collins, M., Miller, F.G., *Do the Brain Dead Merely Appear to be Alive?* 43 J Med. Ethics 747, 751 (2017).

[210] Joffe, A.R., Carcillo, J., et al., *Donation After Cardiocirculatory Death: A Call for a Moratorium Pending Full Public Disclosure and Fully Informed Consent*, 6 Philos Ethics Humanit Med 17 (2011).

false.[211][212][213][214] A body that can still absorb nutrients delivered through veins or undergo puberty cannot be considered dead. Many brain-dead individuals live(d) in vegetative state for several years.[215] If a supposedly brain-dead mother can deliver a child, she was not dead in the first place.[216] Life cannot be equated to higher brain activity or consciousness. An embryo does not develop brain until three weeks of gestation.[217] So, can the embryo be considered alive until then? Is the current definition of abortion capable to encompass this moral and scientific dilemma?

The argument that the brain death cannot be considered as biological death is totally baseless and illogical. UDDA adopts brain death as the legal definition of death. Even though brain dead individuals absorb nutrients, it is made possible through artificial life support. They will not be able to control the basic biological functions on their own. The argument that brain-dead individuals

---

[211] Byrne P.A., et al., *Brain Death: An Opposing Viewpoint*, 242 JAMA 71, 71-80 (1979).
[212] O'Reilly S., et al., *Brain Death: The Patient, the Physician, and Society*, 18 Gon Law Rev. 429, 429-516 (1982).
[213] Evers J.C., et al., *Brain Death: Still a Controversy*, 53 The Pharos of Alpha Omega Alpha 10, 10-12 (1990).
[214] Robert Truog, *Is it Time to Abandon Brain Death?*, 27 Hastings Cent Rep 29, 29-37 (1997).
[215] Pallis, C., *Whole Brain Death Reconsidered: Physiological Facts and Philosophy*, 9 J. Med Ethics 32, 35 (1983).
[216] Field, D.R., et al., *Maternal Brain Death During Pregnancy: medical and Ethical Issues*, 260 JAMA 816, 862 (1988).
[217] Konkel, Lindsay, *The Brain Before Birth: Using fMRI to Explore the Secrets of Fetal Neurodevelopment*, 126 E.P.H. 1,2 (2018).

have lived in a vegetative state is a fallacy, because there is clear scientific evidence to highlight the distinction between vegetative state and brain death.[218] Again, a brain-dead mother is able to deliver the child because she is on life support.[219][220] A brain dead mother was found incapable to exercise her constitutional right to refuse treatment and terminate pregnancy as she no longer had the consciousness to exercise the privacy rights.[221] Even though it is scientifically true that an embryo does not develop a brain until three weeks of gestation, the beginning of life is not demarcated with the development of brain cells. This argument has been used in the abortion debate; however, it has no place in the realm of brain death.[222][223] Brain death can only occur when an individual has a fully developed brain.

Wikler mocks at the philosophers and scientists who advocate for allowing brain-dead patients to die. He points out the irony in their arguments as a

---

[218] Ian Keith McDaniel, Life and Death Issues in Bioethics: Abortion, Persistent Vegetative State, and the Definition of Death (Dec. 4, 2015) (Ph.D. dissertation, University of Kansas) (on file with author).

[219] *Id.*

[220] Daniel Sperling, *Should a Patient who is Pregnant and Brain Dead Receive Life Support, Despite Objection from Her Appointed Surrogate?*, 22 AMA J Ethics e1004, e1005 (2020).

[221] University Health Services v. Piazzi, Richmond County No. CV86-RCCV-464 (1986).

[222] Kushner T., *Having a Life Versus Being Alive*, 10 J Med Ethics 5, 5-8 (1984).

[223] Gareth J., *The Problematic Symmetry Between Brain Birth and Brain Death*, 24 J Med Ethics 237, 237-242 (1998).

dead person cannot die again.[224] Proponents argue that we violate the rights of a brain-dead person when we force her to continue on life-support. If brain death was actual death, will a dead person be legally competent to exercise fundamental rights? He argues that even the proponents of brain death are unsure about the reliability of the concept. Alan Shewmon was an arduous advocate of brain death, but his own experiments and trials proved otherwise, and he changed his position on the topic.[225] He argues that cessation of whole brain function may imply the stoppage of brain activity, but not the end or loss of life.[226] Some Catholic bioethicists even call brain death a conspiracy.[227]

But Wikler's argument has an inherent problem – the wrong use of terms and language. Proponents of brain death advocate for withdrawal of life support and declaration of legal death of patients who are brain-dead. Similarly, Shewmon's perspectives have not been universally accepted by the legal and medical communities. His views are not based on verifiable empirical data.[228] Tonti-Filippini, a Catholic Bioethicist argues that when the brain activity stops, an individual loses the purpose of

---

[224] Wikler, D. et al., *Editorial*, 261 JAMA 2246, 2247 (1989).

[225] Robert Spaemann, *Is Brain Death the Death of a Human Person?* In LOVE AND THE DIGNITY OF HUMAN LIFE: ON NATURE AND NATURAL LAW 45-69 (Eerdmans, B., ed., 2012).

[226] Shewmon, D.A., *Chronic Brain Death*, 51 Neurol. 1538, 1538-1539 (1998).

[227] Byrne P.A., et al., *Brain Death is False*, 66 Linacre 42, 48 (1999).

[228] Patrick Lee, German Grisez, *Total Brain Death: A Reply to Alan Shewmon*, 26 Bioethics 275, 275-284 (2010).

human life, and that she should be considered dead even if the body functions mechanically.[229] Medical guidelines across the country mandate that once death is determined, all medical interventions must be terminated.[230][231] [232] A physician has not duty to treat when the patient is dead.[233][234] A person is not a patient once she is dead.[235][236] Wouldn't the continual of interventions on a dead individual constitute assault or maltreatment of the corpse?[237] Wouldn't the physician be criminally liable for the abuse of the corpse?[238] To disregard the brain death standard

[229] Nicholas Tonti-Filippini, *You Only Die Twice: Augustine, Aquinas, the Council of Vienne, and Death by the Brain Criterion*, 38 Communio 308, 308-325 (2011).

[230] JOINT COMMITTEE ON BIOMEDICAL ETHICS OF THE LOS ANGELES COUNTY MEDICAL ASSOCIATION & LOS ANGELES COUNTY BAR ASSOCIATION, GUIDELINES FOR PHYSICIANS: FORGOING LIFE-SUSTAINING TREATMENT FOR ADULT PATIENTS (2006).

[231] American Academy of Pediatrics, *Clinical Report: Guidelines for the Determination of Brain Death in Infants and Children: An Update of the 1987 Task Force Recommendations*, 128 PEDIATRICS e720 (2011).

[232] D.M. Shaner et al., Really, *Most SINCERELY Dead: Policy and Procedure in the Diagnosis of Death by Neurologic Criteria*, 62 Neurol. 1683 (2004).

[233] PETER SINGER, RETHINKING LIFE AND DEATH: THE COLLAPSE OF OUR TRADITIONAL ETHICS 22 (1994).

[234] See, e.g., Gallups v. Cotter, 534 So.2d 585 (Ala. 1988); Lovato v. District Court, 601 P.2d 1072 (Colo. 1979); Dority v. Superior Court, 145 Cal. App.3d 273 (Cal. App. 1983).

[235] Douglas v. Janssen Funeral Homes, No. 2KB-09-173CI, 2010 WL 9069780, 6-7 (Alaska Super. Ct., Nov. 19, 2010).

[236] M.J. Clarke et al., *Beyond Transplantation: Considering Brain Death As a Hard Clinical Endpoint*, 14 AM. J. BIOETHICS 43, 43-45 (2014).

[237] J.A. Anderson et al., *Refusal of Brain Death Diagnosis: The Health Lawyer's Perspective*, 9 JONAS HEALTH CARE L. ETHICS & REG. 90 (2007).

[238] Range v. Douglas, 763 F.3d 573, 588 (6th Cir. 2014).

would mean to remain blind to the scientific and medical innovations and discoveries.[239] Brain death standard has been developed after thorough and foolproof examination of scientific data and has been legally recognized by statute and case laws.[240][241][242] A recent case determined by the Ontario Consent and Capacity Board[243] in Canada serves as a good guiding example for the United States. This Board resolves disputes between family and clinicians over treatment decisions. In two separate incidents, two individuals were killed, and the physicians determined to withdraw life support. However, their family opposed the clinical decision. The Board declared that the conflict does not involve the issue of treatment, because as the individuals are legally dead, any treatment carried out on them are mere mechanical processes performed on a corpse.[244]

---

[239] Lovato v. District Court In and For Tenth Judicial Dist., 198 Colo. 419, 425 (1979).

[240] Brophy v. New England Sinai Hospital, Inc., 497 N.E.2d 626 (Mass. 1986).

[241] In re Storar, 52 N.Y.2d 363 (1981).

[242] State v. Olson, 435 N.W.2d 530 (1989).

[243] Gabriel B., Pope T., et al., *Reason-giving and Medical Futility: Contrasting Legal and Social Discourse in the United States with the United Kingdom and Ontario, Canada*, 150 CHEST J. 714, 716 (2016).

[244] In re UH (Ont. CCB Oct 28, 2016); In re EI (Ont. CCB Sep. 30, 2016) (Can.).

Argument 2: The lack of uniform diagnostic criteria is problematic as it makes brain death determination unreliable.

There is no universal consensus about the concept.[245][246] It is often cited that brain death criteria were not developed scientifically.[247] No information on clinical trials were cited when Harvard published the criteria.[248] Minnesota criteria was developed on the basis of a study conducted by observing just 25 patients.[249] There is no requirement to perform an EEG in the criteria followed by U.K.[250] The flexibility of the inconsistent criteria raises concerns amongst several clinicians, philosophers, and legal scholars.[251]

Even though there is no consistency in the criteria to determine brain death, several countries have accepted and legislated certain medical standards to diagnose death. Harvard criteria was developed after thorough assessment and deliberations on

---

[245] Wijdicks, E.F.M., *Brain Death Worldwide: Accepted Fact but No Global Consensus in Diagnostic Criteria*, 58 Neurol. 20, 23 (2002).

[246] Swash, M., et al., *Brain Death: Still-Unresolved Issues Worldwide*, 58 Neurol. 9, 9-10 (2002).

[247] Paul A. Byrne, Walt F. Weaver, *Brain Death is not Death*, *in* BRAIN DEATH AND DISORDERS OF CONSCIOUSNESS 43-44 (Machado and Shewmon ed., 2004).

[248] *Id.*

[249] Mohandas, A. et al., *A Clinical and Pathological Study*, 35 J Neurosurg. 211, 211-218 (1971).

[250] AN APPRAISAL OF THE CRITERIA OF CEREBRAL DEATH: A SUMMARY STATEMENT, JAMA (1977).

[251] Walker, A.E., *Cerebral Death*, *in* 2 THE CLINICAL NEUROSCIENCES 75, 75-89 (Chase T.N. ed., 1975).

scientific evidence and expert opinions.[252] Similarly, Minnesota criteria was developed by a large multidisciplinary panel that consisted of physicians, medical experts, legal scholars, and bioethicists.[253] Both these panels combined clinical experience, medical knowledge, and legal scholarship. Even though U.K. does not mandatorily require the clinicians to perform an EEG as an ancillary test, the absence of EEG results do not invalidate brain death.

The opponents often argue that the inconsistent diagnostic standards to determine brain death raises doubts about its reliability. Josef argues that the medical criteria to determine brain death is absurd.[254] He points out that if brain death is determined by the inability to breathe spontaneously, then any person on artificial life-support would be considered dead.[255] Ambiguity in such an important medical determination cannot be tolerated by a civilized society.[256] Uniform clinical testing practices are required because determination of death should be made definitively.[257]

---

[252] Erin Barnes, et al., *Inconsistency in Brain Death Determination Should not be Tolerated*, 22 AMA J Ethics e1027, e1027-e1032 (2020).

[253] *Id.*

[254] Seifert, Josef, *Is Brain Death Actually Death?*, 76 The Monist 175, 176 (1993).

[255] *Id.*

[256] *Id.* at 177.

[257] Greer D.M., Robinson J.D., et al., *Variability of Brain Death Policies in the United States*, 73 Neurol 213, 214 (2016).

Variability of protocols cannot discredit or nullify a scientific fact. UDDA has specifically outlined the diagnostic criteria, and this serves as the legal yardstick to determine death.[258] Calling the brain death standard is not acceptable. It is vital to understand the possibility of mismatches and mathematical inaccuracy in the diagnostic tests.[259] It is not possible to conclusively ascertain when life transitions to death.[260][261] Additionally, protocols may vary across healthcare systems and socio-cultural contexts.[262]

The absence of regular cycles of sleep and wakefulness should not be the reason to determine the death of a person, because even a continuous vegetative state is called wakeful unawareness.[263] If the absence of voluntary mobility is a criterion to declare brain death, then aren't quadriplegic individuals functioning human beings?[264] Vague criteria cannot be used to make decisions about life and death.[265] Even among advocates of brain death, there are several differences in the arguments. Some argue that death happens when the entire brain

---

[258] *See supra note* 252.

[259] *See supra note* 259.

[260] *Id.*

[261] Bernat J.L., *On Irreversibility as a Prerequisite for Brain Death Determination*, 550 Adv. Exp Med Biol. 161, 161-167 (2004).

[262] *See supra note* 252.

[263] Lukas J.M., *The Demise of Brain Death*, 73 BJPS 487, 491 (2022).

[264] *Id.* at 492.

[265] *Id.* at 503.

stops functioning.[266] Some others argue that death happens when just the neocortex inside the brain stops working.[267]

It is important to note that the absence of regular sleep cycles is not the sole criterion to determine brain death. It is one among the different aspects taken into consideration. Likewise, absence of voluntary mobility is not the only criterion involved in the diagnostic standards. The variations in the arguments of the proponents of brain death do not undermine the validity of the concept.

The Uniform Law Commission has been debating several revisions to the UDDA.[268] One among the proposed changes is replacing the current brain-death standard of the permanent stoppage of brain or respiratory functions with a criteria where persistent coma and loss of brainstem reflexes could be used to declare death.[269] The proposal seeks to remove the criterion of irreversibility and replace it with permanency.[270] Several religious groups and bioethicists have come forward opposing

---

[266] Winston Chiong, *Brain Death Without Definitions*, 35 Hastings Cent Rep 20, 21 (2005).

[267] *Id.*

[268] UNIFORM LAW COMMISSION, SESSION RESOURCES (2023) (on file with the author).

[269] *Id.*

[270] *Id.*

this proposal.[271][272] Byrne argues that the proposed change would remove the possibility of performing apnea and all ancillary tests that seek to ensure accuracy. He equates the proposal with involuntary euthanasia.[273]

The proposed change would actually align the legal standard with the neurorespiratory criteria.[274] The accusations of Byrne raise concerns because he perpetuates misinformation and arguments that are not supported by scientific evidence. Brain death criteria has nothing to do with involuntary euthanasia. Brain death determination is made after several strict standard tests and examinations. There are no involuntary actions involved. So, there is no room for the slippery slope in brain death. Each case is different, and clinicians follow the legally required steps before certifying brain death of a patient.

Peter Singer argues that the current criteria to determine death needs to be devised as none of

---

[271] Daniel Payne, *U.S. Bishops Warn Against Proposed Change to Definition of Death*, CAN (Jul. 20, 2023, 09:12 AM), https://www.ncregister.com/cna/u-s-bishops-warn-against-proposed-change-to-definition-of-brain-death.

[272] Letter from the National Catholic Bioethics Center to the Uniform Determination of Death Committee of the Uniform Law Commission (Jul. 12, 2023) https://www.usccb.org/resources/Joint_submission_NCBC_and_USCCB_on_UDDA_2023.pdf.

[273] *Proposed UDDA Revisions Expand law that Allows Euthanasia of Organ Donors*, ANGLICANS FOR LIFE, https://anglicansforlife.org/2023/05/31/proposed-udda-revisions-expand-law-that-allows-euthanasia-of-organ-donors/ (May 31, 2023).

[274] *See supra note* 48.

the tests give a definitive result.[275] He also argues that the current legal definition of death in the U.S. itself is vague that harvesting organs may potentially be charged as murder.[276] He accuses that the proponents of brain death have never given a satisfactory answer on why they focus on brain activity to determine death.[277] He calls their arguments illogical and fallible as an oyster that has no brain, live and die, and to associate brain with life or death is not founded on scientific reasoning or logic.[278]

Singer's comparison of human beings with oysters is oversimplified and irrational. The biological structures of human life are different from that of organisms like oysters. Also, the human brain is the center of control for all bodily functions. So, this comparison itself is wrong. There is nearly unanimous consensus of the medical community that when the whole brain no longer functions, the person is dead. In addition, the prevailing practice of the medical community nationwide is to regard total brain death as the death of the person.[279]

Argument 3: Brain death determination does not respect the dignity and personhood of the

---

[275] Peter Singer, *The Challenge of Brain Death for the Sanctity of Life Ethic*, 8 Ethic & Bioethic 153, 158 (2018).
[276] *Id.*
[277] *Id.*
[278] *Id.* at 162.
[279] In re Haymer, 115 III. App.3d 349 (1983).

individual. It often violates the principle of informed consent.

Josef argues that brain death creates a disconnect between personhood and existence.[280] There needs to be clarity in the arguments of the proponents about how they define being alive. He questions whether human mind indicates consciousness which is tied to the brain functions or human mind has a separate existence from the brain.[281] He opines that mind-related tissues cannot be said to be situated entirely inside the brain, as he believes in the separation of spiritual and biological existences.[282]

While Joseph raises a valid question about personhood and existence, it is vital to note that brainstem reflexes do not constitute personhood. The concept of personhood is complex and multifarious. There are no measurable criteria to determine the loss or destruction of personhood because it is a philosophical notion. The personhood argument may be used in the moral debates surrounding life and death; however, it falls short when meted out against scientific facts. In legal settings, the concept of personhood may vary as per circumstances and contexts. The distinction between spiritual and biological existences do not go hand in hand with the scientific foundations of brain death.

---

[280] *See supra note* 7.

[281] *Id.* at 179.

[282] *Id.*

Spaemann argues that the unity of atomic life and the state of being alive constitutes actual life, and death occurs when this unity is disintegrated.[283] He relies on the principle of *ens et unum convertuntur* (being and unity are convertible).[284] Death and life can never be truly defined.[285] He condemns the horrible experiments meted out on animals to analyze the true nature of pain in the 1600s and argues that scientists tried to challenge normal human perceptions. Scientists tried to prove that pain is just a mechanical reaction of the body. He draws an analogy between these horrible experiments and the attempts to redefine death.[286] If we cannot call the stoppage of heartbeat as the destruction of the organ itself, it is unethical and illogical to term brain death as the destruction of brain functions.[287] He concludes his famous research work by stating that when in doubt, presume that the person is alive.[288]

While Spaemann has contributed to the scholarship of moral deliberations on brain death, the definition of death is not a metaphysical issue in this context. Law and medicine override his arguments. In medicine, determination of life and death is made based on objective criteria. His presumption may not always be applicable in medico-legal settings. For instance, if an individual or her surrogate

[283] *See supra note* 225.
[284] *Id.*
[285] *Id.*
[286] *Id.*
[287] *See supra note* 247.
[288] *See supra note* 225.

decision maker has consented to withdrawal of life support or brain death determination, the physician has to respect the wishes rather than presuming the patient is alive or attempting to save her. Further, his comparison of animal experiments to the determination of brain death is not quite analogous. Those experiments had no role in the current understanding of brain death.

The American Academy of Neurology has repeatedly published statements that physicians need not obtain informed consent before they determine brain death.[289] Many physicians argue that providing treatment to brain-dead patients is futile. However, if the patient is alive as per law, such treatment cannot be considered futile or medically inappropriate.[290] Even if it results in overutilization of limited resources, physicians are in no position to develop a policy for resource allocation.[291] Physicians' failure to respect the wishes of the surrogate decision makers will increase the distrust among the public.[292] Several studies and surveys indicate that neurologists, particularly pediatric neurologists opine that they do not need consent

---

[289] BRAIN DEATH, THE DETERMINATION OF BRAIN DEATH, AND MEMBER GUIDANCE FOR BRAIN DEATH ACCOMODATION REQUESTS: AAN POSITION STATEMENT, AMERICAN ACADEMY FOR NEUROLOGY (2019).

[290] Brittany M. Lee, et al., *Can a Parent Refuse the Brain Death Examination?*, 145 Pediatric 2340, 2345 (2020).

[291] *Id.*

[292] *Id.*

before performing apnea test.[293][294] A court in Virginia ruled that consent of the parents or guardians is not required to perform apnea test.[295] Many scholars oppose this idea as it blatantly violates the principle of informed consent.[296] Further, the basic guiding principle of palliative care is to integrate medical care and the wishes of the family members to provide the best quality of care. Any attempt to disregard informed consent would violate the whole concept of palliative care.[297]

Unambiguous evidence of a patient's wishes are needed for the removal of life support.[298] Law has the authority to define the standard of death, and the medical community has the autonomy to determine the applicable criteria as per the accepted medical standards, to determine brain death.[299] A court in Montana recently ruled that DNC has potential repercussions to patients and their family members,

---

[293] Lewis A., Adams N., et al., *Organ Support after Death by Neurologic Criteria: Results of a Survey of U.S. Neurologists*, 87 Neurol. 827, 827-834 (2016).

[294] Lewis A., Adams N., et al., *Organ Support after Death by Neurologic Criteria in Pediatric Patients*, 45 Crit Care Med e916, e916-e925 (2017).

[295] In re Lawson v. VCU Medical Center, No. CL16-2358 (2016).

[296] Robert D. Truog, et al., *Counterpoint: Should Informed Consent be Required for Apnea Testing in Patients with Suspected Brain Death? Yes*, 152 Chest. 702, 702-704 (2017).

[297] Papadatou D., Goldman A., et al., *The Team*, *in* TEXTBOOK OF INTERDISCIPLINARY PEDIATRIC PALLIATIVE CARE 55-63 (Wolfe J., ed. 2011).

[298] Cruzan v. Director, Mo. Dept. of Health, 497 U.S. 261 (1990).

[299] In re Welfare of Bowman, 94 Wash.2d 407 (1980).

and that physicians should never perform any tests without informed consent.[300]

Argument 4: Brain death determination places higher emphasis on organ procurement than saving the patient's life. It may reduce the potential for recovery.

It is argued that brain death determination is performed to increase organ donation. Byrne and Weaver argue that brain death was developed by a few academicians to meet the utilitarian needs of organ donation in the 1960s.[301] If the hospital receives consent to perform brain death determination, clinicians will focus on harvesting the organs rather than saving the patient.[302] They even equate declaration of brain death with homicide.[303] Spaemann argues that the interests of the Harvard Commission in formulating a brain death standard are not the patient's interests.[304] The only underlying interests are to offer legal immunity to clinicians who withdraw life support and facilitate organ transplants.[305] Hoffenberg argues that the delirious demand of organs across the world required

---

[300] In re The Guardianship of A.C., No. DE-16-08 (2016).

[301] *See supra note* 287.

[302] *Id.*

[303] *Id.* at 46.

[304] *See supra note* 288.

[305] *Id.*

the development of legal guidelines to provide immunity for physicians against assault.[306]

This argument is flawed because brain death determination is based on detailed diagnostic criteria that have been ratified by law. At the same time, determination of brain death has facilitated legal organ harvesting and saved thousands of lives.[307] Equating brain death determination with homicide is an extreme argument. It is unacceptable to accuse physicians who stringently follow clinical protocols and legal standards to declare brain death. Also, the interest of the Harvard Committee was to clarify the ambiguous nature of brain death and set forth proper guidelines and diagnostic criteria to determine brain death.

Dr. Coimbra performed a clinical trial involving brain-injured animals and identified the varying levels of possible recovery.[308] Most often brain may be stunned due to the injury, and it does not necessarily mean that the person is dead.[309][310] Scientific evidence shows that even a person declared brain dead may still have some part of the

---

[306] Hoffenberg R., *Christiaan Barnard: His First Transplants and Their Impact on Concepts of Death*, 323 BMJ 1478, 1479 (2001).

[307] Lakshmi Kumar, *Brain Death and Care of the Organ Donor* 32 J Anaesthesiol Clin Pharmacol 146, 146-152 (2016).

[308] Coimbra, C.G., *Implications of Ischemic Penumbra for the Diagnosis of Brain Death*, 32 Braz J. Med Biol Res 1479, 1479-1487 (1999).

[309] Kim, S.J., et al., *Persistent Stunning Induces Myocardial Hibernation and Protection – Flow/Function and Metabolic Mechanisms*, 92 Circ Res 1233 (2003).

[310] Parmar, G., Lalani A.V., *The Sleeping Heart: Hibernating Myocardium*, 1 Pers. Cardio 44, 44-53 (2001).

brain that functions.[311] However, a large group of clinicians advocate that just because hypothalamus still works, it should not reject the possibility of declaring brain death.[312] It is important to note that organ donation must follow the dead donor rule, which states that the person must be unequivocally dead before organs are harvested.

Comparing a stunned brain with a dead brain oversimplifies brain death determination. While stunned brain may be a temporary state, brain death is permanent and irreversible. Minimal brain function cannot negate the brain death determination because it is based on various criteria. The Dead Donor Rule is a legal and ethical principle that is strictly followed by physicians.[313][314] As brain death is legal death, organ harvesting from brain-dead patients is not a crime.

Truog and Robinson opine that the current concept of brain death is not compatible with the biological or philosophical denominations of death.[315] In their acclaimed work, they predict that the concept of brain death may vanish once organ

---

[311] Michael Nair-Collins, et al., *Hypothalamic-Pituitary Function in Brain Death*, 31 J Intensive Care Med 41, 41-45 (2016).

[312] *See supra note* 289.

[313] Peter J., et al., *Organ Donation: Dead Donor Rule Sets Guidelines For Harvesting Organs*, 46 Opthal Times 1, 1-3 (2021).

[314] Gail A., Van Norman, *A Matter of Life and Death: What Every Anesthesiologist Should Know about the Medical, Legal, and Ethical Aspects of Declaring Brain Death*, 91 Anesthesiol 275, 275-277 (1999).

[315] Robert Truog, Robinson W.M., *Role of Brain Death and the Dead Donor Rule in the Ethics of Organ Transplantation*, 31 Crit Care Med 2391, 2391-2392 (2003).

transplants become popular and the public no longer look for the adherence to the dead donor rule. Their hypothesis is that the brain death standard was created to support the transplantation trade.[316] Potts and Evans back this claim by arguing that the removal of organs is what kills the patients.[317] They further points out the possibility of misusing the pragmatic idea of brain death determination to harvest organs from non-critical patients.[318] They predict a slippery slope where medical professionals forego Hippocratic oath and utilize the lopsided power structure between them and patients to exploit the latter's vulnerability.[319] There are also concerns that apnea test or related ancillary tests may reduce the chances of recovery, especially that of brain tissues.[320]

However, Truog and Robinson also argue that harvesting organs from brain dead people is ethical as they do not have consciousness or chance of recovery.[321] This reflects the contradiction in their research. States have legitimate interests in preventing doctors from assisting their patients to die, even those who are terminally ill or in great

---

316 *Id.*

317 Potts M., Evans D.W., *Does it Matter that Organ Donors are Not Dead? Ethical and Policy Implications*, 31 J Med Ethic 406, 406-407 (2005).

318 *Id.*

319 *Id.*

320 Goudreau J.L., et al., *Complications during Apnea Testing in the Determination of Brain Death: Predisposing Factors*, 55 Neurol. 1045, 1048 (2000).

321 *See supra note* 315.

pain.[322] If the victims were properly diagnosed as dead, of course, no subsequent medical procedure such as the organ removals would be deemed a cause of death.[323] Thus, law protects patients from unauthorized interventions.

[322] Vacco v. Quill, 521 U.S. 793 (1997).
[323] People v. Eulo, 63 N.Y.2d 341 (1984).

CHAPTER

06

CONSCIENTIOUS OBJECTIONS TO BRAIN DEATH: EXPLORING THE HARD CONVERSATION

Conscience does not have a stable definition. It is considered as the consciousness of the ethical righteousness or culpability of an individual's behavior.[324] It is the impression of good and bad ingrained in every individual due to her social existence and is often used synonymously with equity.[325] Even though it is deemed to be the guide to goodness, it is impossible to find unanimity in what can be considered good or bad. Philosophers have rightly pointed out that the human conscience is an individual's unique island[326], the only truth that each person knows[327], and the voice that does not yield to majoritarian views.[328]

Similarly, it is extremely difficult to legally define conscience. The notion of conscience is evoked and interpreted in multiple contexts within private

[324] *Conscience*, MERRIAM-WEBSTER DICTIONARY (11th ed. 2022).
[325] *Conscience*, BLACK'S LAW DICTIONARY (6th ed. 2021).
[326] See, HARPER LEE, GO SET A WATCHMAN (2015).
[327] John Henry Newman, *Conscience Quotes*, NOTABLE QUOTES, http://www.notable-quotes.com/c/conscience_quotes.html.
[328] See, HARPER LEE, TO KILL A MOCKINGBIRD (1960).

law in England[329], including breach of contract, estoppel, forfeiture etc. The dilemma is to determine whether we are evaluating the conscience of an individual based on objective criteria or subjective interpretations of morality. Several legal scholars have opined that law and conscience will remain parallel.[330][331][332] The concept of conscience is explored by the judiciary to ascertain institutional morality of the courts[333], procedural[334] or substantive fairness[335], and similar issues.[336] When dealing with questions related to judicial propriety, the core issue is to assess whether the judge's conscience is incompatible with the law.[337]

Freedom of Conscience in the United States

Despite the inconsistency in the definition of the concept, freedom of conscience is considered to have legal acceptance in the United States. James Madison considered conscience to be the most holy

---

[329] Agnew S., *The Meaning and Significance of Conscience in Private Law*, 77 C.L.J. 479, 479-505 (2018).

[330] H.L.A. HART, THE CONCEPT OF LAW (2nd ed. 1994).

[331] RONALD DWARKIN, TAKING RIGHTS SERIOUSLY (1977).

[332] LON L. FULLER, THE MORALITY OF LAW (1964).

[333] Carnival Leisure Indus v. Aubin, 53 F.3d 716, 719 (5th Cir. 1995).

[334] Brown v. United States, 890 F.2d 1329, 1347 (5th Cir. 1989).

[335] Johnson v. Rodriguez, 943 F.2d 104, 110 (1st Cir. 1991).

[336] See, e.g., Stanley v. Schriro, 598 F.3d 612, 615 (9th Cir. 2010) (court emphasized that in good conscience, it would be unjust to send individuals to death penalty without assuring that their trials were not prejudiced).

[337] *See supra note* 329.

property.[338] Although the First Amendment does not explicitly talk about this freedom, legal scholars opine that it protects the freedom of speech and religion.[339][340] There are three liberties that often seem intertwined but are different. Freedom of thought, conscience, and religion are recognized and shielded under the International Human Rights Law.[341][342] Freedom of thought is described as an individual's fundamental right to have her own opinions and principles without the fear of intrusion or duress from others.[343] Freedom of conscience refers to the basic human right to have one's own values and morals.[344] It need not necessarily be affiliated to religious denominations.[345] Freedom of religion encompasses the right to adopt or believe, practice and engage in religious practices, and express the beliefs without discrimination.[346]

In Europe, freedom of conscience has been generally interpreted in the light of freedom of

---

[338] Bryan Neihart, *What is Freedom of Conscience, and Why Does it Matter?* ALLIANCE DEFENDING FREEDOM, (Apr. 11, 2023), https://adflegal.org/article/what-freedom-conscience-and-why-does-it-matter.

[339] Id.

[340] Clay v. United States, 403 U.S. 698 (1971).

[341] International Covenant on Civil and Political Rights, Dec. 16, 1966, 999 U.N.T.S. 171, art. 18 § 1.

[342] United Nations Declaration on Human Rights, G.A. Res. 217A (III) (UDHR), Dec. 10, 1948, art. 18.

[343] *Id.*

[344] UNITED NATIONS HUMAN RIGHTS OFFICE OF THE HIGH COMMISSIONER, #FAITH4RIGHTS TOOLKIT (2022).

[345] *Id.*

[346] International Covenant on Civil and Political Rights, Dec. 16, 1966, 999 U.N.T.S. 171, art. 18 § 1.

thought.[347] However, freedom of conscience in the United States has been condensed under the freedom of religion in the recent past.[348] The belief in the existence of God rooted in the colonial history of the country has spread a misconception that freedom of conscience and freedom of religion are interchangeable.[349]

Freedom of conscience has found its way into professional settings. For instance, individuals can object to serve in the military if such employment violates their religious or ethical beliefs.[350] This freedom allowed large corporations to deny birth control coverage if the religious beliefs of the owners are against it.[351] A baker can even refuse to create a wedding cake for a homosexual couple.[352] A Catholic foster care invoked this freedom to provide services to homosexual couples.[353] Religious organizations could opt out of mandatory contraceptive care rule under Affordable Care Act if their beliefs are against birth control.[354] Court has struck down a provision that required pro-life institutions to provide

---

[347] PAUL M. TAYLOR, FREEDOM OF RELIGION, UN AND EUROPEAN HUMAN RIGHTS LAW AND PRACTICE (1st ed. 2005).

[348] JOHN WITTE JR. & JOEL A. NICHOLS, RELIGION AND THE AMERICAN CONSTITUTIONAL EXPERIMENT, (3rd ed. 2011).

[349] Rafael Domingo, *Restoring Freedom of Conscience*, 30 J.L. & Relig. 176, 176- 193 (2023).

[350] United States v. Seeger, 380 U.S. 163 (1965).

[351] Burwell v. Hobby Lobby Stores Inc., 573 U.S. 682 (2014).

[352] Masterpiece Cakeshop v. Colorado Civil Rights Commission, 370 P.3d 272 (2018).

[353] Fulton v. City of Philadelphia, 320 F. Supp. 3d 661 (2021).

[354] Little Sisters of the Poor v. Pennsylvania, 591 U.S. __ (2020).

information about abortion care.[355] Pharmacists can object to dispense certain medicines if it violates their religious or moral beliefs.[356]

At the same time, it is vital to analyze how the U.S. judiciary has balanced the freedom of conscience against the freedom of speech and religion. The Supreme Court has held that freedom of conscience does not indemnify harmful and illegal religious practices.[357] The Court also has upheld the supremacy of anti-discrimination laws over religious beliefs.[358][359] Further, if a religious institution uses banned substances in the ceremonies, state can intervene and apply the criminal law, even if it substantially burdened the religious beliefs of the members.[360]

Conscientious Objection in Medicine

Conscientious objection in medicine refers to the denial of providing or accepting medical treatment. It may mean that the healthcare professionals refuse to provide certain procedures, medications, or

---

355 National Institute of Family and Life Advocates v. Becerra, 585 U.S. __ (2018).

356 Stormans, Inc. v. Selecky, 844 F.Supp. 2d 1172 (2015).

357 Reynolds v. United States, 98 U.S. 145 (1879).

358 Arlene's Flowers v. State of Washington, 138 S. Ct. 2671 (2018) (mem.).

359 Harris Funeral Homes v. EEOC, 590 U.S. __ (2020).

360 Employment Division v. Smith, 494 U.S. 872 (1990).

treatments because of ethical reasons.[361][362][363] This should not be confused with medical negligence or malpractice.[364] Most of the states in the United States have developed conscience clauses in their health legislations to protect immunity for healthcare professionals who do not want to provide certain treatments due to their religious or ethical beliefs.[365] Conversely, conscientious objection may also mean that patients refrain from accepting certain medical procedures because they violate their personal beliefs or conscience.

Conscientious objection originally emerged as a religious objection against certain activities like joining the Military.[366] Certain religious groups like Quakers and Jehovah's Witnesses who were against taking a person's life raised religious objections to participate in the wars.[367] They highlighted the importance of upholding one's ethical, religious, or

---

[361] Cynthia J., *Conscientious Objection, Not Refusal: The Power of a Word*, 88 Linacre Q., 242, 242-246 (2021).

[362] Hasan S., *The Challenges of Conscientious Objection in Healthcare*, 55 J Relig Health 384, 384-393 (2016).

[363] Nathan G., Toni S., *A Taxonomy of Conscientious Objection in Healthcare*, 17 Clinical Ethics 63, 63-70 (2022).

[364] *Id.*

[365] Nancy B., *Conscience Clauses, Healthcare Providers, and Parents*, HASTINGS BLOG, (Jun. 30, 2023), https://www.thehastingscenter.org/briefingbook/conscience-clauses-health-care-providers-and-parents/.

[366] John H. Matheson, *Conscientious Objection to Military Service*, THE FIRST AMENDMENT ENCYCLOPEDIA, (Jan. 23, 2009), https://www.mtsu.edu/first-amendment/article/912/conscientious-objection-to-military-service.

[367] *Id.*

personal beliefs.[368] However, very soon this concept began to be applied in the practice of medicine. The same religious groups who advocate for right to life began to use this shield to resist providing sterilization, contraception, and abortion services.[369]

Conscientious Objections: Why are They Better than Religious Exceptions?

Accommodating conscientious objections in the healthcare realm crosses the divides between religious and secularist expressions.[370][371] It has a wider scope because it encompasses diversity of beliefs irrespective of religion.[372][373] This respects the individual autonomy in a secular democracy.[374] This concept attempts to strike a balance between an individual's autonomy and the state's interests, regardless of the nature of the objection.[375] Using religion-based exceptions can be discriminatory.[376]

---

368 *Id.*

369 Sawicki Nadia, *Disentangling Conscience Protections*, 48 Hastings Cent Rep 14, 14-22 (2018).

370 Pellegrino E., *The Physician's Conscience, Conscience Clauses, and Religious Belief: A Catholic Perspective*, 30 Fordham Urban Law J 221, 221-244 (2002).

371 Weinstock D., *Conscientious Refusal and Healthcare Professionals: Does Religion Make a Difference?* 28 Bioethics 8, 8-15 (2014).

372 Savulescu J., *Conscientious Objection in Medicine*, 332 BMJ 294, 294-297 (2006).

373 Alberto G., Savulescu J., *Beyond Money: Conscientious Objection in Medicine as a Conflict of Interests*, 17 J Bioeth Inq. 229, 229-243 (2020).

374 *Id.*

375 Yossi N., *Religious Conscientious Exemptions*, 30 Law Philos. 143, 143-166 (2011).

376 *Id.*

There is a dire need to secularize the freedom of conscience in medicine. This will result in diversity[377], anti-discrimination practices[378], and prioritization of evidence-based care.[379] Thus, secularization of freedom of conscience will enable equal treatment of all objections in the eyes of law.

Conscientious Objection to Brain Death Determination

Brain death determination is a highly contentious topic as it decides if a person is dead or alive. Families often find it very difficult to accept this determination and this may lead to overutilization of resources. Regardless of the negative consequences of the objections to brain death determination, upholding these opinions and objections is vital to ensure patient autonomy. Several religious groups are against the concept of brain death. Individuals who do not follow any particular religion may also oppose the concept because of the discrepancies in the concept and the widespread misconceptions about the determining tests. However, it is very important to accommodate all such objections.[380]

---

[377] Maria Jose Valero, *Freedom of Conscience of Healthcare Professionals and Conscientious Objection in the European Court of Human Rights*, 13 Religions 558, 558 (2022).

[378] U.S. DEPARTMENT OF HEALTH AND HUMAN SERVICES, CONSCIENCE AND RELIGIOUS NON-DISCRIMINATION (2022).

[379] Sean M., Stephen J., *Freedom of Conscience in Healthcare: Distinctions and Limits*, 10 J Bioeth Inq. 347, 347-354 (2013).

[380] Alyson S., *Issues with the Determination of Brain Death: The Case for Religious and Moral Exceptions*, Law School Student Scholarship 1106

New York, California, and Illinois have reasonable accommodation clauses in their death laws. However, the implementation varies. In New York, reasonable accommodation is provided only when the patient has expressed an objection to the determination.[381] California allows for all types of objections, but only for a reasonable period of time after the brain death determination.[382] However, what is the reasonable period is unclear. In reality, this reasonable period is often the 24 hours before the hospital determines to withdraw life support.[383] Even though Illinois statute talks about the need to accommodate the patient's religious beliefs, it does not mandate, rather request to consider such objections.[384]

New Jersey is the only state that allows for a religious/moral objection to the determination of brain death.[385] The law here alters the status of the patient. For instance, a patient dead in New York may be considered alive in New Jersey. If a patient or surrogate decision maker objects to brain death determination, the patient will continue to be placed

(2020).

[381] 10 N.Y.C.R.R. § 400.16 (1987).

[382] CAL. HEALTH & SAFETY CODE § 1254.4 (a) 2012.

[383] *See supra note* 380.

[384] 210 ILL. COMP. STAT. 85/6.23 (2012).

[385] N.J. REV. STAT. § 26:6A-5; N.J. ADMIN. CODE § 13:35-6A.6.

on life support until she dies as per cardiopulmonary criteria.[386][387]

Opponents of the conscience clause in death laws argue that brain death is legal death, and the accommodation of religious and moral objections is equivalent to denial of science and logical reasoning.[388] If a society cannot reach a unanimous opinion on when a person dies, it shall have long-term policy implications.[389] Opponents also argue that death should not have multiple definitions to satisfy the egos and beliefs of a few religious groups.[390]

However, a society must be tolerant to accommodate diverse beliefs and ideas. If there are two sides for similar health issues like end-of-life decision or abortion, it is normal to have multiple opinions about the actual concept of death. Orthodox Jews, certain sects of Islam, Native Americans etc. still abide by the cardiopulmonary criteria of death. Any secular country must be tolerant to these diverse religious beliefs.

---

[386] Eelco Wijdicks, Brain Death, 118 Handb. Clin. Neurol. 191, 191-203 (2013).

[387] Anne L., et al., *Family Members' Requests to Extend Physiologic Support After Declaration of Brain Death: A Case Series Analysis and Proposed Guidelines for Clinical Management*, 25 J. CLIN ETHICS, 222 (2014).

[388] ROBERT M. VEATCH & LAINIE F. ROSS, DEFINING DEATH: THE CASE FOR CHOICE, 116 (1st ed. 2016).

[389] *Id.*

[390] *Id.* at 138.

Arguments against Conscientious Objection

Conscientious objection may harm the patients because they are being denied the access to basic healthcare services.[391] Healthcare professionals are legally bound to provide evidence-based care to the patients and place the well-being of the patients above their personal beliefs.[392] The opponents of conscientious objection in medicine believed that the United States had the potential to become a progressive, secular nation over time.[393] Conscientious objection may be used to perpetuate discrimination against marginalized communities.[394][395] Healthcare professionals may often fail to balance individual autonomy and their professional duties.[396]

Arguments for Conscientious Objection

Conscientious objection must be preserved because it is vital to respect an individual's autonomy and her ethical decisions.[397] Human beings are moral

---

[391] Ishmael Bradley, *Conscientious Objection in Medicine: A Moral Dilemma*, CLINICAL CORRELATIONS, (May. 28, 2009), https://www.clinicalcorrelations.org/2009/05/28/conscientious-objection-in-medicine-a-moral-dilemma/.

[392] Id.

[393] Savulescu J., Schuklenk U., *Doctors Have No Right to Refuse Medical Assistance in Dying, Abortion or Contraception*, 31 Bioethics, 162, 162-170 (2017).

[394] *See supra note* 362.

[395] Bjorn K., Morten M., *Conscientious Objection to Intentional Killing: An Argument for Toleration*, 19 BMC Med Ethics 82, 82-83 (2018).

[396] *See supra note* 394.

[397] WICCLAIR M., CONSCIENTIOUS OBJECTION IN HEALTHCARE: AN ETHICAL ANALYSIS, (1st ed. 2011).

agents, and their ethical beliefs and decisions signify their integrity.[398][399] Respecting conscientious objection emphasizes the significance of embracing diversity in our society.[400] Sometimes, individuals are reluctant to join certain professions because they may feel that their ethical beliefs may not be tolerated by fellow professionals.[401] Allowing conscientious objection removes this obstacle.[402][403]

Disallowing conscientious objection will violate the personal liberty of the healthcare professionals and patients.[404] Prohibition of such objection may also be a blatant violation of the freedom of thought and religion.[405] Conscientious objections are only permitted if the objectors can provide valid reasons for the decisions.[406] The U.S. judiciary has recognized the right to conscientious objection.[407] The right to accept or deny treatment has emanated from the right to privacy.[408]

---

398 *Id.*

399 *See supra note* 370.

400 *See supra note* 397.

401 *Id.*

402 West-Oram P, Buyx A., *Conscientious Objection in Healthcare Provision: A New Dimension*, 30 Bioethics 336, 336-343 (2016).

403 Cowley C., *A Defense of Conscientious Objection in Medicine: A Reply to Schuklenk and Savulescu*, 30 Bioethics 358, 358-364 (2016).

404 *See supra note* 372.

405 *See supra note* 373.

406 Doug McConnell, *Conscientious Objection in Healthcare: Pinning Down the Reasonability View*, 46 J Med Philos. 37, 37-47 (2021).

407 Church of Lukumi Babalu Aye v. City of Hialeah, 508 U.S. 520 (1993).

408 Griswold v. Connecticut, 381 U.S. 479 (1965).

Should there be a reasonability standard?

Liberman argues that there should be a reasonability standard to measure the validity of the conscientious objection against the fundamental duties of the professionals.[409] Card argues that there should be valid reasoning to support the objections.[410] The general consensus among the supporters of conscientious objection is that the objectors should present reasons and explain the rationale behind their ethical decisions.[411] Some scholars also point out that we must weigh the genuineness of a conscientious objection rather than scoping it for its reasonableness.[412] But, this can be detrimental as an individual's objection may be genuine, but also racist or homophobic.[413] There is no objective criteria to evaluate the genuineness of an ethical decision. Courts in secular democracies have taken a neutral stand in these situations. They have held that a court is in no position to decide if a particular belief is central to the practice of a religion.[414][415]

---

[409] Liberman A., *Wrongness, Responsibility and Conscientious Refusal in Healthcare*, 31 Bioethics 495, 495-504 (2017).

[410] Card R., *Reasonability and Conscientious Objection*, 28 Bioethics 320, 320-326 (2014).

[411] Kantymir L., McLeod C., *Justification for Conscience Exemptions in Healthcare*, 28 Bioethics, 16, 16-23 (2014).

[412] Myers C., Woods R., *Conscientious Objection? Yes, But Make Sure It is Genuine*, 7 AJOB 19, 19-20 (2007).

[413] *See supra note* 411.

[414] *See supra note* 360.

[415] Syndicat Northcrest v. Amselem, 2 SCR 551 (2004) (Can.).

CHAPTER

07

CRITICAL ANALYSIS OF THE DETERMINATION OF BRAIN DEATH IN THE UNITED STATES

The UDDA is not a federal statute, it is a model law. The state versions of UDDA are not uniform. A person who is declared brain dead in California may be considered alive in New Jersey. There is no consistency in the accepted medical standards[416] and the consent requirements.[417][418] Law remains rather silent on how to deal with conflicting situations where the family opposes the declaration of death.[419] The model law has not been revised to incorporate the scientific discoveries and technological advancements under the accepted medical standards. In a recent case[420], the Nevada Supreme Court noted that it was unclear whether the Death by Neurologic Criteria (hereinafter referred to as DNC) standard published by the American Academy of Neurology (AAN) was the

[416] Pope, Thaddeus, Bonnie, Richard J., et al., *It's Time to Revise the Uniform Determination of Death Act*, 172 Ann. Intern Med. 143, 143-144 (2020).
[417] In re Allen Callaway, no. DG-16-08 (Pondera County Dist. Ct., Mont. 2016).
[418] In re Mirranda Grace Lawson, no. CL16-2358 (City of Richmond Circuit Court, Va. 2016).
[419] *Supra note* 416.
[420] In re Guardianship of Hailu, 361 P.3d 524 (Nev. 2015).

accepted medical standard. After the judgment was pronounced, AAN issued a statement confirming that the DNC standard they published is the accepted medical standard, and several medical associations supported this statement.[421] Immediately after the publication of the statement, Nevada legislature identified the gaps in the statute, and acknowledged it by incorporating provisions identifying the latest, accepted medical standard to determine death and allowing future scientific advancements published by AAN to be included in the standard.[422] UDDA fails to address the scope and acceptability of religious objections to the withdrawal of life support.[423] So, there is no uniformity in how states deal with religious and/moral objections to the declaration of brain death as death.

The Uniform Law Commission (ULC) has been debating about the need to revise the UDDA since early 2022.[424] The discussion emerged after Thaddeus Pope published the famous article[425] where he initially proposed revisions to UDDA in 2020. Several bioethicists including him argue that clinicians need not obtain family consent to perform

---

[421] Lewis, A., Blosser, S., et al., *An Interdisciplinary Response to Contemporary Concerns about Brain Death Determination*, 90 Neurol. 423, 423-426 (2018).

[422] Nev. Rev. Stat. § 451.007 (2017).

[423] *See supra note* 119.

[424] Adam Kovac, *Inside the Heated Scientific Debate to Redefine Who is Dead*, THE DAILY BEAST (Jul. 6, 2022, 2:42 PM), https://www.thedailybeast.com/inside-the-heated-scientific-debate-to-redefine-who-is-dead.

[425] *See supra note* 420.

diagnostic procedures including the apnea test on a potentially brain-dead patient.[426] They must inform the kins of the patient before performing the diagnostic tests, but the specific consent of family is not required.[427] This proposal has sparked heated debates among bioethicists. Catholic bioethicists and doctors opine that this would amount to blatant violation of patient autonomy. [428] Some doctors point out the possibility of apnea test causing brain swelling in a patient who is not actually brain-dead.[429]

Jason Eberl, a leading catholic bioethicist, points out that the principle of double effect[430] which is central to the Moral theology in catholic beliefs would not apply in this case, as the apnea test is not actually intended to provide any benefits to the patients. Even if we view the proposal through a secular or non-religious lens, not mandating consent of the family (or the surrogate decision-maker) before performing diagnostic tests on the patient to determine the DNC would mean total denial of the basic principles of medical ethics. Over a hundred physicians came forward and published

---

[426] *See supra note* 424.

[427] *Id.*

[428] Lucy Grindon, *Possible Brain Death Law Changes Pose Ethical Concerns*, NATIONAL CATHOLIC REPORTER (May 11, 2021, 2:00 PM), https://www.ncronline.org/news/possible-brain-death-law-changes-pose-ethical-concerns.

[429] *Id.*

[430] *Id.* (explaining the principle of double effect as the doctrine that allows for actions that are potentially harmful as long as we can strike a proportionate balance between the positive and negative effects).

a joint statement against this proposal.[431] They argue that while it is important to have uniformity in brain death laws across the country, there should be an opt-out clause for those who do not necessarily believe in the concept of brain death and have diverging opinions on what death means to them.[432] It would be unjust to discriminatorily impose the opinions of the experts when people may have different religious and cultural beliefs.

This leads us to some substantial questions – Should law offer religious exemptions from the determination of brain death? Is there a basis for providing reasonable accommodations for conscientious objections to the concept of brain death? Whose religious beliefs are we talking about? This issue is a volatile floor of debate. First of all, it is important to acknowledge the fact that even if we bring forth uniformity in the brain death laws, people belonging to different religions may or may not accept brain death as death. Orthodox Jews, some sects of Native Americans and Islam followers, and Buddhists do not accept brain death as a death.

The Constitution guarantees the fundamental right to freely practice one's religion[433] and any law passed in the country must adhere to this

---

[431] D Alan Shewmon, *Statement in Support of Revising the Uniform Determination of Death Act and in Opposition to a Proposed Revision*, J. Med Philos., jhab014 (2021).

[432] *Id.*

[433] U.S. Const. amend. I.

principle. It may be argued that the government has a compelling state interest to bring forth uniformity in brain death laws. It can also be argued that if religious exceptions are provided, this may cripple the societal interest to clearly define life and death.[434] The government, however, is not allowed to impose restrictions on any religious practice unless it can demonstrate that doing so is the least restrictive way to advance a compelling state interest.[435] Further, it has been established that each person has the right to personal autonomy in medical decision-making.[436] This would mean that the patient (or her surrogate decision-maker) must have complete autonomy on whether to perform diagnostic tests and continue life-support even after the clinical determination of brain death. Thus, even the revised form of UDDA should allow for religious objections to the determination of brain death, by incorporating an opt-out clause.

Now, what happens when a brain-dead patient is continued on life-support in a scarce emergency care setting, and a newly admitted terminal patient could be saved from accessing that very life-support? This triage can be solved by law by mandating that the accommodations should be 'reasonable.' Reasonable standard is often defined

---

[434] Chaim, Dovid Z., *Accommodating Religious Objections to Brain Death: Legal Considerations*, 17 JHCS 49, 64-65 (1989).

[435] Thomas v. Review Board of Indiana Employment Security Division, 450 U.S. 707, 718 (1981).

[436] Schloendroff v. Society of New York Hospitals, 211 N.Y. 125, 129-130 (1914).

as the perspective of an impartial spectator.[437] When the physicians and the family of the brain-dead patient may have differing opinions about death, the reasonable view would be to accommodate the conscientious objections.[438]

The standard to declare an accommodation to be unreasonable is pretty high. An accommodation is considered unreasonable if it causes undue hardship including escalating costs to the entity.[439] As of now, New Jersey is the only state that specifically provides under its law that if a patient objects to DNC on religious grounds, then death shall solely be determined by the cardiorespiratory criteria.[440] The law also stops insurers from declining coverage on the basis of brain death if the patient's family objects to DNC.[441]

It is pertinent to note that reasonable accommodations may be sought not only on the basis of religious beliefs, but also on the grounds of cultural differences and distrust in the process due to historical injustices meted out against marginalized communities. Even people who do not follow any particular religion may have their own notions of death. So, the law must not only recognize the religious objections, but also

---

[437] Sibley, W.M., *The Rational versus the Reasonable*, 62 The Phil. Rev. 554, 554-560 (1953).

[438] Johnson, L.S., *The Case for Reasonable Accommodation of Conscientious Objections to Declarations of Brain Death*, 13 Bio. Inq. 105, 105-115 (2016).

[439] 42 U.S.C. § 12111 (10).

[440] NJ L., Ch.90, § 5 26:6A-5 (1991).

[441] *Id.*

the conscientious objections. This may alarm the bioethicists because they will be concerned about widespread rejections of the notion of brain death. Well, this can be addressed only through imparting clear education and implementing equitable health policies to reduce the distrust in the healthcare systems. Providing for reasonable accommodations on the basis of religious and conscientious objections would mean that law and policy recognize and respect the diversity.

Brain death laws in New York[442] and New Jersey[443] seek to respect the religious beliefs of the patient. They turn to the surrogate decision-maker or the patient's family only when the religious beliefs of the patient are not accurately available. So, the primary importance should be given to the beliefs of the patient and in the absence of the same, the family can decide whether or not to consent to diagnostic tests to determine DNC and withdraw life-support.

There have been some bizarre cases of brain death that led the public to question the concept of brain death and challenge that brain dead people are not actually dead. One prominent case is that of Jahi McMath[444], a 13-year-old girl in the State of California whose brain death was declared in 2013, after an oropharyngeal surgery led to a bleeding

[442] NY Comp Codes R & Regs Ch. 10, §400.16.

[443] NJ Admin Code §13:35-6A.6.

[444] Shewmon DA, Salamon N., *The Extraordinary Case of Jahi McMath*, 64 Perspect Biol Med. 457, 457-478 (2021).

disorder. Her family launched a legal battle to continue life-support.[445] The initial suit was filed in Alameda County Superior Court. The court sought expert opinion from the Chief of Child Neurology at Stanford Medical School who reported that Jahi did not show any activity on EEG, and she could not breathe without mechanical ventilation, which all showed that she was brain dead. This led the Alameda Court to rule that Jahi was legally dead in California. The disgruntled family filed an appeal with the Northern District of California's US District Court. While the appeal was ongoing, negotiations between the family and hospital staff resulted in the decision that Jahi would be released to her family's care with mechanical ventilation and life support. She was later taken to New Jersey where she was legally alive, and she remained there until she died due to abdominal and kidney malfunction in 2018. This controversial case fueled the public distrust towards brain death and spread the misconceptions that brain death and cardiac death are separate concepts. This also deepened the distrust in the organ transplant conundrum.

Another case that shook the nation was that of Marlise Munoz.[446] She was a pregnant woman who was declared brain dead in Texas. However, the Texas law mandated that she should be kept on life-

[445] Winkfield v. Children's Hospital Oakland, (N.D. Cal. Jan 22. 2014).

[446] Tom Dart, *Texas Hospital Acknowledges Brain Dead Status of Pregnant Woman*, THE GUARDIAN (Jan. 24, 2014, 4:43 PM), https://www.theguardian.com/world/2014/jan/24/texas-hospital-acknowledges-brain-dead-pregnant-woman.

support because she was pregnant. Her husband initiated a legal action[447] to remove her from life-support as that was her wish and belief. The Texas law restricted the application of advance directives of pregnant women, but her husband argued that she was legally dead, and that this restriction has no validity in the instant case. The court ruled in his favor and ordered the hospital to remove Munoz's life-support.[448] There have been cases where brain dead patients delivered healthy babies.[449][450] All these instances have questioned the underlying basis of DNC. At the same time, some scholars and neurologists have pointed out that these cases were simply false positives of brain death diagnoses.[451]

In light of these aforementioned cases, a key issue that emerged in the recent past is the need to redefine the criteria to determine death. Some bioethicists have proposed that the legal criteria must keep pace with the latest medical standards.[452]

---

[447] Erick Munoz v. John Peter Smith Hospital (Cause No. 096-270080-14) (2014).

[448] Ed Lavandera, *Texas Judge: Remove Brain-Dead Woman from Ventilator, Other Machines*, CNN HEALTH (Jan. 24, 2014, 10:09 PM), https://www.cnn.com/2014/01/24/health/pregnant-brain-dead-woman-texas/.

[449] Ian Austen, *Brain-Dead: A Canadian Woman Remains a Silent Partner Awaiting Birth*, THE N.Y. TIMES (Feb. 6, 2014, 6:45 PM), https://www.nytimes.com/2014/02/07/world/americas/brain-dead-a-canadian-woman-lives-on-as-a-silent-partner-awaiting-birth.html.

[450] Paula Newton, *Brain-Dead Canadian Woman Dies after Son's Birth*, CNN HEALTH (Feb. 12, 2014, 7:32 AM), https://www.cnn.com/2014/02/11/health/canada-brain-dead-pregnant-woman/index.html.

[451] *Supra note* 444.

[452] Adam, Omelianchuk, Art, Caplan, et al., *Revise the UDDA to Align the Law with Practice through Neurorespiratory Criteria*, 98 Neurol. 532, 532-

They contend that there is a global agreement among medical professionals to redefine the DNC as the total and irreversible loss of brain function as indicated by an unresponsive coma with the absence of awareness, brainstem reflexes, and independent breathing.[453] They call it the Neurorespiratory Criteria.[454] According to the academics, adding neurorespiratory criteria to the UDDA will base the determination of death on the loss of critical functions.[455] The existing criteria emphasizes on anatomical mortality.[456] Some argue that brain-dead patients attain puberty, menstruate, and even deliver babies, and this calls for including the diagnosis of hormonal functions to assess brain death.[457]

It is essential to read bioethics in the light of the politics of race. Implicit bias against people of color in healthcare settings should not be overlooked when it comes to the determination of death. Michele Goodwin pointed out the one-sided analyses and opinions perpetuated by bioethicists in Jahi McMath's case.[458] Jahi McMath was Black. Her family's cultural and religious beliefs stopped them from accepting the notion that brain death is death. She menstruated, moved her hips and arms

---

536 (2022).

453 *See supra note* 207.

454 *Id.*

455 *See supra note* 452.

456 *Id.*

457 Robert D. Truog, *The Uncertain Future of the Determination of Brain Death*, 329 JAMA. 971, 971-972 (2023).

458 Goodwin, Michele, *Implicit Bias and the Case of Jahi McMath*, 48 Hastings Cent. Rep., S77, S77-S78 (2018).

(as a reflex), her skin was warm, and she breathed.[459] They believed that she was alive. Seldom did the scholars discuss what led to the sudden stoppage of her heart amidst the treatment. The ENT team did not intervene when she was profusely bleeding after the initial procedure, the doctor on duty frowned upon the family, and the nurses did not complete the notes.[460] The family lamented that Jahi would have gotten more attention, care, and respect if she was white.[461] The doctors, bioethicists, and public health scholars stubbornly tried to force the family to accept her death. Some of the remarks made by the leading bioethicists were brutal.[462] Some argued that she will start to decompose, and that it is wrong to keep a dead body on life support, and most of them called the family crazy.[463][464] Yes, the law considers brain death to be death. But most of the scholars missed (or rather ignored) the opportunity to address the systemic racism in healthcare. They failed to discuss how the physicians and the

---

[459] *Id.*

[460] Rachel Aviv, *What does it mean to Die?* THE NEW YORKER (Jan. 29, 2018, 10:03 AM), https://www.newyorker.com/magazine/2018/02/05/what-does-it-mean-to-die.

[461] *Id.*

[462] Los Angeles Times Staff, *Jahi McMath: Expert Criticizes keeping Girl on Ventilator*, LA TIMES (Jan. 13, 2014, 12:00 PM), https://www.latimes.com/local/lanow/la-xpm-2014-jan-13-la-me-ln-jahi-mcmath-ventilator-20140113-story.html.

[463] Jason Wells, *Jahi McMath is Brain Dead; Hopes for Life are Futile: Experts Say*, LA TIMES (Dec. 13, 2013, 12:00 PM), https://www.latimes.com/local/lanow/la-xpm-2013-dec-30-la-me-ln-jahi-mcmath-case-misconceptions-20131230-story.html.

[464] Caplan, A., Magnus, David, *Brain Death is Really Death*, TIME (Jan. 3, 2014, 5:45 AM), https://time.com/194/brain-death-really-is-death/.

healthcare professionals interacted with the Black family. They failed to acknowledge the underlying cultural differences and beliefs. And, when they failed, the white racial privilege once again reigned over the realm of bioethics. This is one of the reasons why people of color still have deep distrust towards healthcare.

CHAPTER

08

COMPARATIVE ANALYSIS OF BRAIN DEATH LAWS IN THE UNITED STATES AND INDIA

Colonialism is a system that enforced apartheid[465], genocide[466], racism[467], and all forms of exploitation.[468] The effects of colonialism still persist in the 21st century. It is rightfully said that colonialism never went away, rather evolved.[469][470] Both the U.S. and India share the dark history of colonialism. Although the U.S. became independent from the British empire in 1776, India could only gain independence in 1947. Being governed by the same ruler during the colonial era, both these countries adopted the common law system. U.S. and India are democracies, with written constitutions. Both the constitutions have adopted the separation of

---

465 Gorelick, R.E., *Apartheid and Colonialism*, 19 CILSA 70, 70-71 (1986).

466 DIRK MODES & DAN STONE, COLONIALISM AND GENOCIDE 7 (2007).

467 CAROLINE ELKINS, LEGACY OF VIOLENCE: A HISTORY OF THE BRITISH EMPIRE 12 (2022).

468 Bigon, L., Njoh, A.J., *Power and Social Control in Settler and Exploitation Colonies: The Experience of New France and French Colonial Africa*, 53 JAAS 932, 935 (2018).

469 Michelle Garcia-Olp, *How Colonization Impacts Identity through the Generations: A Closer Look at Historical Trauma and Education* (Aug. 1, 2018) (Ph.D. dissertation, University of Denver) (on file with author).

470 Helene Caux, *Effects of Colonialism Still being Felt to this Day*, U.N. NEWS (Feb. 18, 2022), https://news.un.org/en/story/2022/02/1112292.

powers doctrine, checks and balances between the different branches of the government, and a similar set of fundamental rights. In fact, the members of the drafting committee of the Indian Constitution adopted several features of the U.S. Constitution including the due process clause.

However, the models of federalism adopted by both the countries are different and unique. The Indian Constitution has both unitary and federal features. Thus, India has a quasi-federal system of government. The key federal features include the supremacy of the written Constitution, elaborate amendment procedures, and division of powers between the national and regional governments. The main unitary features include the centralizing tendencies of the national government, single citizenship[471], and unified judiciary.[472] U.S. has a federal system of government. It follows dual federalism, where both the federal and state governments have separate spheres of autonomy. The form of government in the U.S. emphasizes on a Presidential rule, however Prime Minister is the de facto head of the Indian government. A judge in the U.S. can hold the office as long she is deemed fit. However, in India, judges of different courts have age limits for retirement. The amendment of the U.S. Constitution is formal and inflexible.[473] Even though the procedure to amend the Indian

[471] *See supra note* 151, Art. 5 – 11.
[472] *Id.* Art. 124 – 147.
[473] U.S. Const. art. V.

Constitution[474] is lengthy, it has been amended more than 100 times in the past 75 years. This reflects the flexibility of the Indian Constitution to adapt to the changes in the society. The law-making process in India involves introduction of a bill, publication and public input, and passage and assent.[475] The law-making process in the U.S.[476] involves introduction of a bill, committee review, floor debate and voting, conference committee review, and presidential approval.

Despite having rules to regulate brain death determination, the legal and ethical arguments presented in support of this concept vary in India and the U.S., owing to the differences in history, culture, beliefs, societal infrastructure, and legal systems. Thus, it is pivotal to compare and contrast the laws governing brain death in both the countries. India does not have a separate, comprehensive law to regulate brain death. It is mentioned in THOTA, however the provision to determine brain death is seldom evoked. U.S. has a comprehensive model legislation that governs the determination of brain death, called the UDDA. Both the countries define brain death similarly. Both of them have laws that facilitate and regulate organ donation after determination of brain death. But there are significant differences in the approaches adopted by them. India follows the U.K. concept of

---

[474] *Id.* Art. 368.

[475] *Id.* Art. 245 – 255.

[476] *See supra note* 8. art. I.

brainstem death.[477] U.S. has adopted a whole-brain definition of death, which requires cessation of all brain functions.[478] There are no state-based laws in India that govern determination of brain death. Only the State of Kerala introduced an ordinance to implement a Standard Operating Procedure[479] for uniform determination of brain death across the State. There are significant conflicts over what the accepted clinical standards are in the United States. However, the policymakers in India have not yet attempted to define the accepted medical standards which complicates the controversy over brain death determination.

The Case for DNR: Why India needs to act immediately?

An advanced directive is a legal document that is prepared in advance to determine medical decisions for an individual.[480] It is a written statement whereby an individual expresses the extent of treatment she wishes to obtain, the nature of medical interventions that she is willing to accept, and sometimes the end-of-life decisions.[481] It can

---

[477] Dhanwate, D. Anant, *Brainstem Death: A Comprehensive Review in the Indian Perspective*, 18 IJCCM, 596, 597 (2014).

[478] *See supra note* 114.

[479] *See supra note* 188.

[480] Steven House, Caroline Schoo, et al., Advance Directives, STATPEARLS (Jan. 20, 2023), https://www.ncbi.nlm.nih.gov/books/NBK459133/.

[481] *Id.*

be either general or specific in nature.[482] It may also authorize another person to take the medical decisions if the individual loses her capacity.[483] The concept of advance directives originated from the principle of self-determination.[484] Advance directive respects the dignity and autonomy of the patient.[485] The option to add a surrogate decision maker highlights how the law recognizes and places value upon the individuality, dignity, autonomy, and beneficence of the patient.[486] The two most common types of advance directives are the durable power of attorney[487] and the living will.[488] The power of attorney, otherwise known as a healthcare surrogate is an individual who is authorized to take medical decisions on behalf of the patient who has been incapacitated due to illness.[489] The living will may

---

[482] *Advance Directives and Surrogate Decision Making*, CENTER FOR HEALTH ETHICS, (Jul. 3, 2023, 10:11 AM), https://medicine.missouri.edu/centers-institutes-labs/health-ethics/faq/advance-directives.

[483] *Id.*

[484] Eva Winkler, *Do Researchers in Empirical Ethics Studies Have a Duty to Act Upon their Findings? Case Study in End-of-Life Decision Making*, 14 J Empir Res Hum Res Ethics 438, 438-439 (2019).

[485] Donald Kollisch, Robert Santulli, et al., *The Limits of Advance Directives in Maintaining Autonomy in Patients with Advanced Dementia*, 134 Am J Med 963, 963-967 (2021).

[486] M.J. Newton, *Precedent Autonomy: Life-Sustaining Intervention and the Demented Patient*, 8 Camb Q Healthc Ethics 189, 189-199 (1999).

[487] Arvind Venkat, Julianna Becker, *The Effect of Statutory Limitations on the Authority of Substitute Decision Makers on the Care of Patients in the Intensive Care Unit: Case Examples and Review of State Laws Affecting Withdrawing or Withholding Life-Sustaining Treatment*, 29 J Intensive Care Med. 71, 71-80 (2014).

[488] Robert Orr, Autonomy, Conscience, and Professional Obligation, 15 Virtual Mentor 244, 244-248 (2013).

[489] *Id.*

or may not appoint a healthcare surrogate. It rather states the choices of medical interventions and the end-of-life treatment decisions.[490]

A Do Not Resuscitate (DNR) order is a document that identifies the patient's wishes to deny resuscitating treatments.[491] This is a written order by the patient, that is countersigned by the healthcare provider.[492] The physicians are legally obliged to follow the DNR order.[493] It is vital to identify the role of DNR in brain death diagnosis. Although DNR orders may not directly affect brain death determination, they may offer an opportunity to optimally allocate the resources in healthcare settings.[494] DNR orders also facilitate organ transplants.[495] DNR orders form the primary mechanism to identify and honor the wishes of the patient who does not want aggressive medical interventions.[496] Another new form of advance directive is the Physician's Orders for Life-Sustaining Treatment (POLST).[497] It is a joint agreement between the physician and the patient. The physician and patient discuss various treatment

[490] *Id.*

[491] Claude Hemphill, *Do Not Resuscitate Orders, Unintended Consequences, and the Ripple Effects*, 11 Crit Care 121, 121 (2007).

[492] *Id.*

[493] *Id.*

[494] Osamu Muramoto, *Informed Consent for the Diagnosis of Brain Death: A Conceptual Argument*, 11 Philos Ethics Humanit Med s13010, s13016 (2016).

[495] John Lizza, *Why DCD Donors are Dead*, 45 J Med Philos 42, 42-45 (2020).

[496] *Id.*

[497] *See supra note* 480.

options, beliefs, and wishes regarding end-of-life decisions. The physician thereafter summarizes and records them as medical orders.[498] However, a POLST cannot be enforced if it contradicts the living will.[499]

Advance directives are not enforced blindly. They are only valid if the patient executed them in actual capacity.[500] The patient must comprehend and understand the information, compare treatment options against beliefs and values, and communicate the preferences very clearly.[501][502] At present, we have several options that can be incorporated in an advanced directive, including DNR, Do Not Intubate, Palliative Care, Do Not Hospitalize, Resuscitate, Trial of Treatment, and Hospice Care.[503]

United States regulates advance directives through a combination of state and federal laws. The Patient Self-Determination Act (PSDA) mandates that all providers who participate in Medicare and Medicaid must provide information about advance directives to the patients.[504] However, studies show

---

498 *Id.*

499 *Id.*

500 Eileen Baker, Catherine Marco, *Advance Directives in the Emergency Department*, 1 J Am Coll Emerg Physicians Open. 270, 270-275 (2020).

501 *Id.*

502 Jennifer Bertkau, Lori Herbst, *Ethics of Pediatric and Young Adult Medical Decision-Making: Case-Based Discussions Exploring Consent, Capacity, and Surrogate Decision Making*, 17 MedEdPORTAL 11094, 11094 (2021).

503 Abdelmalek C., Goyal S., et al., *Advance Directives: Give Teeth to End-of-Life Choices*, 6 Aging Well 24, 24-27 (2013).

504 Pub. L. No. 101-508, 104 Stat. 1388-115 (1990).

that only 31 percent of the patients complete and submit the advance directive forms.[505] Low literacy rates, language barriers, and lack of awareness are some of the factors contributing to the low completion rates.[506] People also fear that advance directives may lead to poor quality of care.[507] Other federal laws that govern advance care planning are the National Defense Authorization Act[508] and the Medicare Improvements for Patients and Providers Act.[509] States have the autonomy to decide how the incapacitated patients can enforce their wishes with regard to medical care.[510] The concept and definitions of incapacitation vary among states.[511] Congress intends that if the state laws are more prescriptive than the federal regulations, providers must follow their state laws.[512][513]

In India, advance medical directive is a relatively new concept, that has not yet been popularized.[514]

---

[505] Cohen A., Nirenberg A., *Current Practices in Advance Care Planning: Implications for Oncology Nurses*, 15 CJON 547, 547-553 (2011).

[506] Bianca Miller, *Nurses in the Know: The History and Future of Advance Directives*, 22 OJIN 57, 57 (2017).

[507] *Id.*

[508] §748 of P.L. 104-106; 10 U.S.C. 1044c (1990).

[509] P.L. 110-275 (2008).

[510] Clark E., *Healthcare Decision Making and Declarations in New York*, wings.buffalo.edu/faculty/research/bioethics/case.html. (2004).

[511] *Id.*

[512] *Id.*

[513] DeJohn P., *New CMS Guidelines Suggest Changes in Advance Directive Policies*, 29 OR Manager 1,1 (2013).

[514] Prashanth Ram, Vikram Jain, *Living Will: Advance Medical Directive Enabling Dignity of Life in India*, THE IMPACT LAWYERS, (Jan. 14, 2021), https://theimpactlawyers.com/articles/living-will-advance-medical-directive-enabling-dignity-of-life-in-india.

The concept of 'living will' was first discussed in Common Cause v. Union of India[515], wherein the Supreme Court issued directions on how terminally ill patients can execute advance directives about treatment options. The court noted that advance directives may not always be linked to end-of-life decisions, thus dismantling the misconception about advance care planning.[516] In Gian Kaur *v.* State of Punjab[517], court upheld the right to die with dignity. However, there is no legal framework to govern or regulate DNR orders. Although some hospitals consider DNR orders, there is no unified regulation to standardize the practice.[518] Even after the determination of brain death, withdrawal of life support or organ retrieval largely depend on the consent of the family members.[519] There needs to be a legislation to govern DNR orders because this can facilitate brain death determination.[520] Most often, the individual's wishes are overridden by the wishes of the family because of the lack of DNR framework. This may result in futile treatment of the brain-dead patient that is unethical and uneconomical.[521] Thus, it is important that India creates a comprehensive

[515] (2018) 5 SCC 1 (Ind.).

[516] *Id.*

[517] (1996) 2 SCC 648 (Ind.).

[518] *See supra note* 514.

[519] Harsh Deora, Nishant Yagnick, *The Legal Void Outside Brain Death in India: The Legislative Need of DNR in Brain Death*, 71 Neurol India 20, 20-27 (2023).

[520] *Id.*

[521] *Id.*

legal framework to promote, regulate, and govern DNR orders.

Lessons from the SOP: What can the United States do better?

The SOP published by Kerala has a precise set of clinical guidelines to be followed by the medical committee when they ascertain brain death. The steps are provided in a chronological order that enables the physicians to make an accurate diagnosis of death. Each step has to be flawlessly recorded. As the SOP was issued by a state ordinance, it is uniformly applicable across the state, which ensures that all hospitals follow the exact same procedure.[522] The SOP also has clauses to instruct the physicians about the brain death certification process. This will eliminate any confusion that may arise during clinical decisions. It also aims to develop comprehensive public awareness programs to initiate open conversations about life and death and clear any doubts that the public may have regarding the determination of brain death.[523] This will also resolve the fear surrounding organ donation and transplants.[524]

---

[522] *See supra note* 479.

[523] *Id.*

[524] Janani Sampath, *Kerala Shows Way With SOPs for Brain Death Certification*, THE FEDERAL, (Feb. 15, 2020, 7:10 AM), https://thefederal.com/health/kerala-shows-way-with-standard-operating-procedure-for-brain-death-certification/.

If the United States adopt a similar approach, it will enable the country to standardize the diagnosis and certification of brain death. It will ensure that all patients are administered the same tests to determine death. If the Federal Government devises a similar step-by-step procedure, it will reduce the chances of false diagnoses. It will streamline the organ donation procedures. Finally, the physicians and the public will gain clarity over the subject and will override the misinformation being spread by the media.

However, adopting the SOP or similar guidelines may not be easy in the United States due to several reasons. First, all states may have to adopt a similar legal framework, or the Federal Government may have to intervene and devise a uniform framework for the entire country.[525] Coordinating State and Federal Governments may not be easy, given the current political circumstances. Second, the cultural differences need to be taken into consideration. It will be challenging to develop guidelines that may be accepted by all communities. Third, if there are no legal consequences to non-compliance, physicians may not always follow the guidelines consistently.[526]

---

[525] STUP. R., STANDARD OPERATING PROCEDURES: A WRITING GUIDE (2001).

[526] Gidey Amare, *Reviewing the Values of a Standard Operating Procedure*, 22 Ethip J Health Sci. 205, 205-208 (2012).

Illustration Courtesy: *Aswath C. (India)*

CHAPTER 09

FUTURE DIRECTIONS AND EMERGING TECHNOLOGIES

Exploring future directions in brain death and end-of-life technologies is imperative for varied reasons. First, there should be legal clarity to implement effective guidelines and frameworks to keep up with the developments. Second, this exploration is vital to stay prepared for the complex ethical issues that may follow. Third, there is already a considerable amount of confusion regarding the protocols to be followed in brain death determination. So, it is important to have a clear idea about the direction in which healthcare professionals should proceed. Fourth, understanding the potential future of these technologies will prepare the policymakers and educators to develop and incorporate cultural competence and sensitivity into the curriculum of medical schools. This would create awareness about the upcoming technologies, different religious and cultural views about their application, and prepare the future healthcare professionals to be mindful and supportive of the diverse views of patients and families. This in turn can improve the quality and outcomes of healthcare delivery.

AI created a major shift in healthcare in the 21st century.[527][528] It is now replacing manual systems with automated services and resources.[529] AI can now handle simple administrative activities to complex diagnosis and treatment plan recommendations.[530] This is made possible through machine learning, which is the statistical method to create delivery models and train those models by interpreting existing data.[531] There are several forms of AI, but machine learning has been the game changer. Machine learning allows us to enhance precision medicine[532], predict if a patient may acquire a specific disease based on the existing/developing symptoms[533], and interpret radiology data accurately.[534] Deep learning, which is a subset

---

[527] *Use of AI in Healthcare and Medicine is Booming – Here's How the Medical Field is Benefiting from AI in 2021 and Beyond*, INSIDER, (Jan. 11, 2023), https://www.insiderintelligence.com/insights/artificial-intelligence-healthcare/.

[528] *No Longer Science Fiction, AI and Robotics are Transforming Healthcare*, PwC, (May. 30, 2023), https://www.pwc.com/gx/en/industries/healthcare/publications/ai-robotics-new-health/transforming-healthcare.html#:~:text=It%20puts%20consumers%20in%20control,and%20support%20for%20staying%20healthy.

[529] Sri Sunarti, Ferry F. Rahman, et al., *Artificial Intelligence in Healthcare: Opportunities and Risk for Future*, 35 Gaceta Sanitaria S67, S68-S70 (2021).

[530] Thomas Davenport, Ravi Kalakota, *The Potential for Artificial Intelligence in Healthcare*, 6 Future Healthc J. 94, 94 (2019).

[531] *Id.*

[532] Safiye Celik, Scott M. Lundberg, *A Machine Learning Approach to Integrate Big Data for Precision Medicine in Acute Myeloid Leukemia*, 9 Nat Commun. 42, 42 (2018).

[533] *Id.*

[534] Alanna Vial, David Stirling, et al., *The Role of Deep Learning and Radiomic Feature Extraction in Cancer-Specific Predictive Modelling: A Review*, 7 Transl Cancer Res 803, 803-816 (2018).

of machine learning enables identification of patterns and interpretation of big data.[535] Another domain of machine learning is Natural Language Processing (NLP). This technique can detect both linguistic and statistical language.[536] For instance, doctors can converse with patients who speak a different language and understand all their health concerns.[537] Similarly, NLP can create clinical notes of patients and cross-reference it with all possible published research in the area to provide an accurate diagnosis.[538][539]

AI is also being used in the form of physical robots to perform surgery[540] and robotic process automation to perform administrative tasks.[541] Studies show that machine learning apps can even detect underlying psychiatric conditions and prevent suicides.[542][543] Machine learning algorithms

---

[535] Yu B., Beam A., *Artificial Intelligence in Healthcare*, 2 Nature Biomed Eng. 719, 719-721 (2018).

[536] *See supra note* 530.

[537] *Id.*

[538] *Id.*

[539] Hayden Field, *IBM Takes Another Shot at Watson as A.I. Boom Picks Up Steam*, CNBC NEWS (May 9, 2023, 06:00 AM), https://www.cnbc.com/2023/05/09/ibm-takes-another-shot-at-watson-as-ai-boom-picks-up-steam.html.

[540] Thomas Davenport, John Glaser, *Just-in-Time Delivery Comes to Knowledge Management*, 80 Harv Bus Rev. 107, 107-111 (2002).

[541] Hussain A., Malik A., et al., *The Use of Robotics in Surgery: A Review*, 68 Int J Clin Pract. 1376, 1376-1382 (2014).

[542] Chandler C., Foltz P., et al., *Using Machine Learning in Psychiatry: The Need to Establish a Framework that Nurture Trustworthiness*, 46 Schizophr Bull 11, 11-14 (2020).

[543] Kulkarni S., Reddy N. et al., *Facial Expression (Mood) Recognition from Facial Images using Committee Neural Networks*, 8 Biomed Eng. Online

are the ones that read, manage, and interpret personal health information stored on wearable devices.[544] Thus, AI has revolutionized every aspect of healthcare. It is impossible to discuss all AI-related advancements in diagnostic techniques, so the researcher focuses on 2 specific technologies, whose analysis can lead to a generalized overview of the future of brain death determination.

Cryonics and OrganEx – Challenging the notions of death

Cryonics refers to the process of delaying or pausing the dying process by storing the human remains below freezing temperature.[545] The low temperature delays metabolism and stops chemical changes in the bodies.[546] Majority of the scientific and medical community view this practice as substandard method or pseudoscience.[547] Many scientists opine that this controversial practice gives false hope to the patients and families.[548] OrganEx is a recent

16, 16 (2009).

[544] *Supra note* 535.

[545] Benjamin Best, *Scientific Justification of Cryonics Practice*, 11 Rejuvenation Res. 493, 494 (2008).

[546] *Id.*

[547] Steinback R.L., *Mainstream Science is Frosty Over Keeping the Dead on Ice*, CHICAGO TRIBUNE, (Jul. 17, 2019, 12:00 AM), https://www.chicagotribune.com/news/ct-xpm-2002-09-29-0209290429-story.html.

[548] Laurie Clarke, *Why the Sci-Fi Dream of Cryonics Never Died*, MIT TECHNOLOGY REVIEW, (Oct. 24, 2022), https://www.technologyreview.com/2022/10/14/1060951/cryonics-sci-fi-freezing-bodies/.

technology[549][550] developed in the United States that attempts to restore cellular activity in dead pigs.[551][552] During the experiment, a mixture of fluids were injected to the dead pigs which promoted cellular regeneration.[553] The involuntary movements of the heads and necks of the pigs reflected the preservation and restoration of motor functions.[554]

Both cryonics and OrganEx challenge the existing notions and definitions of death.[555] Claudio argues that these technologies alter the concept of death as a singular, momentary occurrence and poses death to be a process or a series of events.[556] It is unclear whether the person is legally dead

[549] Joel Achenbach, *Scientists Restore Some Brain Cell Functions in Pigs Four Hours After Death*, THE WASH. POST, (Apr. 17, 2019, 1:00 PM), https://www.washingtonpost.com/science/2019/04/17/scientists-restore-some-brain-cell-functions-pigs-four-hours-after-death/.

[550] Katie Hunt, *Researchers Revive Cells in Pig Organs Hour After Animal's Death: What This Could Mean for Humans?* ABC NEWS, (Aug. 4, 2022), https://abc7ny.com/yale-dead-pigs-pig-research-organex-brought-back-to-life/12097812/.

[551] Paige Carlson, *Pigs Escape Death by New Technology in Organ Revival*, PORK, (Aug. 4, 2022), https://www.porkbusiness.com/news/industry/pigs-escape-death-new-technology-organ-revival.

[552] Amy Cheng, *The Pigs Had Been Dead for an Hour: Scientists Made Their Hearts Beat Again*, THE WASH. POST, (Aug. 4, 2022, 05:22 AM), https://www.washingtonpost.com/science/2022/08/04/yale-organex-dead-pigs-revived/.

[553] *Id.*

[554] *Id.*

[555] Claudio Cohen, Bioethicists Must Rethink the Concept of Death: *The Idea of Brain Death is not Appropriate for Cryopreservation*, 67 Clinics Sao Paulo 93, 93-94 (2012).

[556] *Id.*

or alive during cryopreservation.[557] Cryonicists believe that the preserved animals or human beings are legally alive.[558] They consider that a person who is being cryopreserved is resuscitated from deanimation.[559] Similarly, OrganEx challenges the notion that cardiac death is irreversible.[560] Some scholars argue that cryonics and OrganEx cannot be used to determine brain death diagnosis. However, research shows that the pigs under OrganEx experiment could not exhibit brain activity because of a neuronal suppressant used in the fluids.[561]

There is uncertainty on how these technologies may be used in large scale to preserve human life. Regardless of the direction in which these technologies are growing, they have altered our perceptions of mortality.[562] Some philosophers and scholars predict that death may ultimately become an administrative process, whereby some families can afford to reverse death, and some others do not have access to these technologies.[563] Scientists may even develop synthetic parts of the brain in the

---

[557] Whetstine L. Streat S., et al., *Pro/Con Ethics Debate: When is Dead Really Dead*, 9 Critical Care 538, 538-540 (2005).

[558] *Id.*

[559] *Id.*

[560] Larry Celegans, *OrganEx Team Revives Dead Pig's Organs: Implications for Cryonics*, LONGEVITY (Aug. 12, 2022), https://www.longevitydao.net/blog-posts/reviving-pigs-cryonics.

[561] *Id.*

[562] Richard Gibson, *The Ethics of OrganEx*, BMJ BLOG, (Aug. 12, 2022), https://blogs.bmj.com/medical-ethics/2022/08/12/the-ethics-of-organex/.

[563] Raiany Romanni, *Technology Promises to Change the Meaning of Death: At Least for Some*, THE WASH. POST, (Aug. 19, 2022, 10:19 AM), https://

future.[564] As outlined in the previous chapters, death still continues to be a subjective, ethical judgment rather than a universally accepted biological truth.[565] Even though these technologies are tempting, they are still being explored, tested, and developed. They may in the future, revive a person who is declared dead, and prolong the average lifespan of human beings. Cryonics may increase the market supply of transplantable organs as cryopreserved organs can last up to centuries.[566] OrganEx can improve treatment outcomes of cardiac patients and detect early symptoms of stroke.[567] Organs treated through OrganEx showed lesser signs of cell damage and tissue swelling.[568] This technology also has the potential to reduce clotting issues during organ transplants.[569]

---

www.washingtonpost.com/outlook/2022/08/19/organex-yale-death-definition-medical-disparities/.

[564] *Id.*

[565] Robert Truog, *Death is Universal, But Sometimes Murky*, THE HARVARD GAZETTE, (Jul. 24, 2018), https://news.harvard.edu/gazette/story/2018/07/harvard-ethicist-robert-truog-on-why-brain-death-remains-controversial/.

[566] Carla Bleiker, *OrganEx Tells Cells Not to Die*, DW (Aug. 3, 2022), https://www.dw.com/en/organex-may-save-donor-organs-by-telling-cells-not-to-die/a-62697834.

[567] Forest Simon, *Pig Cells Restored Through Death-Defying OrganEx Technology*, GENENG NEWS, (Aug. 4, 2022), https://www.genengnews.com/news/pig-cells-restored-through-death-defying-organex-technology/.

[568] Rhiannon Williams, *Researchers Repaired Cells in Damaged Pig Organs an Hour after the Animal's Death*, MIT TECHNOLOGY REVIEW, (Aug. 3, 2022), https://www.technologyreview.com/2022/08/03/1056664/repair-cells-damaged-pig-organs-death-ethics-heart-brain/.

[569] Ricki Lewis, *OrganEx Revives Pigs an Hour after Death, Holding Promise for Transplants*, PLOS BLOGS, (Aug. 4, 2022), https://dnascience.

It is vital to determine the potential ethical implications of these technologies in brain death diagnosis. Cryopreservation may preserve the cells, but the quality or utility of those cells may not be sufficient enough to restore life.[570] It is pertinent to note that a cryopreserved individual is dead according to law, even though the cryonicists may claim otherwise.[571] This dilemma is not new. There is still no consensus on the living status of a frozen embryo.[572] While some may consider it as a potential person, others may view it as a non-living thing until implanted in a uterus.[573] The reanimation of cells is often misconstrued as resurrection.[574] The application of OrganEx and cryonics challenges the existing legal definitions of death. It blurs the fine line between life and death. Cryopreservation of a legally dead brain can have disastrous consequences, whereby resistance against brain death concept may increase tremendously. There is no definite law or judicial decision that talks about the personhood or rights of cryopreserved individuals. In such a situation, harvesting organs from a corpse may become murder in some societies.[575]

---

plos.org/2022/08/04/organex-revives-pigs-an-hour-after-death-holding-promise-for-transplants/.

[570] *See supra note* 555.

[571] *Id.*

[572] *Id.*

[573] *Id.*

[574] *Id.*

[575] *Id.*

Unconscious Bias in AI

AI can predict the mathematical probability of survival or premature death of the patient.[576] Deep learning techniques utilize electronic health record (EHR) data to create personalized treatment plans. This predictive modeling has the potential to guide allocation of limited resources in a hospital. But most of the data fed to the systems are generic and prone to prejudice and bias of the developers and algorithms. To further complicate the problem, the AI industry lacks diversity.[577] This can cause rippling effects. This is analogous to the problems caused by lack of diversity in clinical trials. If the data sets used to create the algorithms do not reflect the diversity in the society, they will not work in actual healthcare settings.[578]

If the model is trained with a person who speaks perfect accent of any language, it may not be able to detect and analyze the different slangs, diction, or pronunciation of minority communities who may

---

[576] Stephen Weng, Luiz Vaz, et al., *Prediction of Premature All-Cause Mortality: A Prospective General Population Cohort Study Comparing Machine-Learning and Standard Epidemiological Approaches*, 14 PLos One e0214365 (2019).

[577] Elise Reuter, *5 Takeaways from the FDA's List of AI-enabled Medical Devices*, MED TECH DIVE (Nov. 7, 2022, 09:30 AM), https://www.medtechdive.com/news/FDA-AI-ML-medical-devices-5-takeaways/635908/.

[578] Amit Kaushal, Russ Altman, et al., Geographic Distribution of U.S. Cohorts Used to Train Deep Learning Algorithms, 324 JAMA 1212, 1213 (2020).

speak differently.[579] Several studies have shown that AI may adapt and learn from the personality traits of the developers and may even turn racist and homophobic.[580][581] Flawed data sets and homogeneity of the professionals have caused AI to be prejudicial.

An application developed by Google started to identify Black people as gorillas due to the flawed data sets.[582][583] When a foster-care system attempted to use AI to detect child endangerment, the tool mostly identified people of color as potential perpetrators.[584] The implicit bias in pain treatment has also been infiltrated into the machine learning models.[585] An algorithm trained with data of White patients to detect melanoma failed to diagnose the disease in the people of color.[586]

---

579 Jack Clark, *Artificial Intelligence has a Sea of Dudes Problem*, BLOOMBERG TERMINAL, (Jun. 27, 2016), https://www.bloomberg.com/professional/blog/artificial-intelligence-sea-dudes-problem/.

580 *Id.*

581 Scott Deveau, Jing Cao, *Microsoft Apologizes After Twitter Chat Bot Experiment Goes Awry*, BLOOMBERG, (Mar. 25, 2016, 04:31 PM), https://www.bloomberg.com/news/articles/2016-03-25/microsoft-apologizes-after-twitter-chat-bot-experiment-goes-awry?in_source=embedded-checkout-banner.

582 *Id.*

583 Kate Crawford, *Artificial Intelligence's White Guy Problem*, N.Y. TIMES, (Jun. 25, 2016, 10:11 AM), https://www.nytimes.com/2016/06/26/opinion/sunday/artificial-intelligences-white-guy-problem.html.

584 VIRGINIA EUBANKS, AUTOMATING INEQUALITY (St. Martin's Press, 2018).

585 *Id.*

586 Adewole Adamson, Avery Smith, *Machine Learning and Healthcare Disparities in Dermatology*, 154 JAMA Dermatol 1247, 1248 (2018).

Bias in AI can cause significant challenges to objective brain death determination. If the training data is non-diverse or misrepresentative of the patient population, the AI system may deliver wrong diagnoses.[587] Such algorithms may also reinforce biases and societal prejudices.[588] If healthcare professionals blindly rely on those flawed algorithms, they may amplify their confirmation bias.[589] For instance, the physician may not give much attention to minor evidence that contradicts her prior assessment.[590] The psychological theory of Dunning-Kruger effect needs to be highlighted in this context. People do not recognize their own mistakes because they deny or ignore the fact that they are fallible.[591] Algorithms that do not adequately represent the patient demographics may exacerbate inequities.[592]

Regulation of AI

Machine Learning or AI-powered medical devices are regulated by the Food and Drug Administration

---

587 Natalia Norori, Qiyang Hu, et al., *Addressing Bias in Big Data and AI for Healthcare: A Call for Open Science*, 2 PATTERNS NY 100347 (2021).

588 *Id.*

589 Donald Redelmeier, Damon Scales, *Missing the Diagnosis of Brain Death as a Self-Erasing Error*, 192 Am J Respir Crit Care Med 280, 280-282 (2015).

590 *Id.*

591 Dunning D., Johnson K., et al., *Why People Fail to Recognize Their own Incompetence*, 12 Curr Dir Pyschol Sci 83, 83-87 (2003).

592 Shania Kennedy, *AI in Medical Imaging May Amplify Biases, Inequities*, HEALTH IT ANALYTICS, (May 3, 2023), https://healthitanalytics.com/news/ai-in-medical-imaging-may-amplify-biases-inequities.

(FDA) in the United States.[593] The traditional approach to approve devices do not go well with the constantly changing and updated devices.[594] So, FDA has changed its approach by introducing new guidelines and guidance sheets.[595][596][597][598] The new framework offers a faster way to get the devices approved once the manufacturers submit detailed information regarding the modifications or updates, methodology deployed, and an impact assessment.[599]

Recently, FDA approved over 90 AI-based medical devices and tools in 2022.[600] FDA also conceived a Digital Health Center of Excellence to regulate digital health technology, including

---

[593] Phoebe Clark, Jayne Kim, et al., *Marketing and US Food and Drug Administration Clearance of Artificial Intelligence and Machine Learning Enabled Software in and as Medical Devices: A Systematic Review*, 6 JAMA Netw Open e2321792 (2023).

[594] Jessa Boubker, Nathan Beaver, et al., *FDA's New Guidance Proposes Flexible Use of AI in Medical Devices*, FOLEY (May 10, 2023), https://www.foley.com/en/insights/publications/2023/05/fdas-guidance-flexible-use-ai-medical-devices.

[595] *Id.*

[596] *Marketing Submission Recommendations for a Predetermined Change Control Plan for Artificial Intelligence/Machine Learning- Enabled Device Software Functions*, FDA (Apr. 2023), https://www.fda.gov/regulatory-information/search-fda-guidance-documents/marketing-submission-recommendations-predetermined-change-control-plan-artificial.

[597] *Proposed Regulatory Framework for Modifications to Artificial Intelligence/Machine Learning Based Software as a Medical Device: Discussion Paper*, FDA, https://www.fda.gov/media/122535/download.

[598] *Artificial Intelligence/Machine Learning-Based Software as a Medical Device Action Plan*, FDA, https://www.fda.gov/media/145022/download.

[599] *See supra note* 594.

[600] *See supra note* 577.

wearable and mobile health devices.[601] 96 percent of the healthcare devices have 510(k) clearance under the 21st Century Cures Act. Such devices need not go through clinical trials if the creators or developers are able to prove that those devices are substantially similar to the ones in the market.[602] The devices with such clearance do not come under the purview of FDA.[603] The rationale behind this clearance is that such devices do not provide a prognosis and treatment suggestions.[604] However, recent advancements have enabled certain smartwatches to predict or detect stroke, sepsis, or embolism.[605] These tools are now being pushed to a gray area where regulation is uncertain. Although FDA has constantly tried to keep up with the rapid technological advancements, the traditional paradigm of regulation was not created with the future of AI in mind.[606]

In India, the regulation of AI-powered medical devices is not unified. Until 2018, these devices were left largely unregulated. This is because over

---

[601] *FDA Launches the Digital Health Center of Excellence*, FDA News Release (Sep. 22, 2020) https://www.fda.gov/news-events/press-announcements/fda-launches-digital-health-center-excellence.

[602] *See supra note* 600.

[603] *Id.*

[604] Elise Reuter, *Software to Predict Risk of Sepsis, Stroke Should be Regulated as a Medical Device*, Says FDA, MED TECH DIVE (Oct. 11, 2022, 10:12 AM), https://www.medtechdive.com/news/fda-regulate-sepsis-software/633732/.

[605] *Id.*

[606] Mahika Ahluwalia, *Legal Governance of Brain Data Derived from Artificial Intelligence*, 7 Voices in Bioethics 1, 1-3 (2021).

70 percent of such devices are imported.[607] The only law in place to regulate the devices was the Drug and Cosmetics Act, 1940,[608] which was further extended in 2017 by the introduction of Medical Device Rules.[609] The new set of rules merely stated that medical devices shall be considered as subset of drugs under the Act.[610] It did not delve into data protection.[611] Another set of rules were introduced in 2020 to regulate multiple aspects of medical devices ranging from processing or manufacturing to marketing.[612] Although this move received a lot of praise from the health law experts, there is incoherence in the language used in the rules which hampers its effective implementation.[613] For instance, clinical investigation and clinical performance plans are not explicitly differentiated.[614] Devices do not require a comprehensive pre-marketing safety data for registration. There is no government database where the public can access the information related to the medical devices.[615]

---

[607] Manas Manu, Gaurav Anand, *A Review of Medical Device Regulations in India, Comparison with European Union and Way-Ahead*, 13 Perspect Clin Res. 3, 3-4 (2022).

[608] Act No. 23/1940 (Ind.).

[609] Damini Sharma, Amrish Chandra, *Medical Device Rules – 2017, India: An Insight*, 7 Appl. Clin. Res. Clin. Trials Regul. Aff. 126, 126-134 (2020).

[610] *Id.*

[611] *Id.*

[612] See, generally, Medical Devices (Amendment) Rules, 2020 (Ind.) https://cdsco.gov.in/opencms/opencms/en/Medical-Device-Diagnostics/Medical-Device-Diagnostics/.

[613] See supra note 607.

[614] *Id.*

[615] *Id.*

Both India and the United States need to create more comprehensive and stringent regulations for AI-powered medical devices and their potential future versions. India needs to lay down detailed guidelines and establish standards to regulate the devices and health data. India can adopt the FDA framework as a starter or foundation. United States must make sure that the FDA regulations continue to grow and evolve to meet the future technologies.[616] FDA can adopt a risk-based approach to regulate AI.[617]

---

[616] Michele Buenafe, *The FDA Regulatory Landscape for AI in Medical Devices*, MED DEVICE ONLINE (Mar. 3, 2023), https://www.meddeviceonline.com/doc/the-fda-regulatory-landscape-for-ai-in-medical-devices-0001.

[617] *Id.*

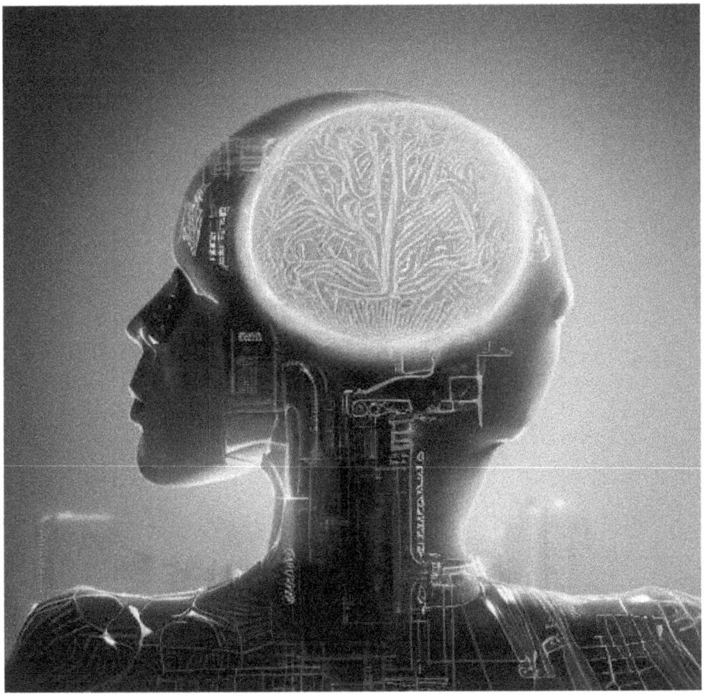

Illustration Generated through deepai.org; Permitted for commercial use

CHAPTER 10

REDEFINING THE POLICY OF BRAIN DEATH IN THE UNITED STATES

"Nothing on this entire globe can be as definite and conclusive as death and taxes."[618]

Even though there is a general consensus in the diagnostic framework to determine brain death, the standards vary among countries, and even states. The lack of uniformity in the criteria to determine brain death is problematic and alarming.[619][620] The inconsistences in the criteria may question the legitimacy of organ transplants.[621][622] The incongruity in the legal and clinical criteria jeopardizes public trust in healthcare.[623][624]

---

[618] Fred Shapiro, *Quotes Uncovered: Death and Taxes*, FREAKONOMICS (Feb. 12, 2011, 1:30 PM), http://freakonomics.com/2011/02/17/quotes-uncovered-death-and-taxes/.

[619] *See supra note* 252.

[620] Lewis A., Bonnie R.J., et al., *It is Time to Revise the Uniform Determination of Death Act*, 172 Ann Intern med 143, 144 (2020).

[621] *See supra note* 618.

[622] Nathaniel M.R., James L.B., *What Should We Do About the Mismatch Between Legal Criteria for Death and How Brain Death is Diagnosed?*, 22 AMA J Ethics e1038, e1040 (2020).

[623] Bernat J.L., *Controversies in Defining and Determining Death in Critical Care*, 9 Nat Rev Neurol 164, 164-173 (2013).

[624] *See supra note* 421.

The law sets forth whole-brain criteria that emphasizes on irreversibility, however the current clinical practices are not sufficient to determine the irreversible stoppage of brain function.[625] The current clinical practices usually focus on the permanent stoppage of circulation and respiration that do not require any proof of irreversible nature of the loss of brain function. The brain death determination may not always successfully differentiate a stunned brain and a permanently damaged brain.[626] Scholars point out the possibility of misdiagnosing a hypo perfused brain with an irreversibly damaged brain.[627][628][629] Hypo perfusion means the deprivation of oxygenated blood. It may occur due to a major brain injury or ischemic stroke. The tests for both these conditions may potentially reveal similar results.[630][631] A recent clinical study performed on pig brains revealed that certain level of cellular function was able to be restored after postmortem.[632] It is true that all cells of brain need not be dead in order

---

[625] Bernat J.L., *On Noncongruence Between the Concept and Determination of Death*, 43 Hastings Cent Rep 25, 25-33 (2013).

[626] Shewmon D.A., *Truly Reconciling the Case of Jahi McMath*, 29 Neurocrit Care 165, 165-170 (2018).

[627] *Id.*

[628] Dalle Ave A.L., Bernat J.L., *Inconsistences Between the Criterion and Tests for Brain Death*, 35 J Intensive Care Med 772, 772-780 (2020).

[629] Astrup J., Symon L., et al., *Thresholds in Cerebral Ischemia: The Ischemic Penumbra*, 12 Stroke 723, 723-725 (1981).

[630] Coimbra C.G., *Implications of Ischemic Penumbra for the Diagnosis of Brain Death* 32 Braz J Med Biol Res. 1479, 1479-1487 (1999).

[631] Daniele S.G., Silbereis J., et al., *Restoration of Brain Circulation and Cellular Functions Hours Post-Mortem*, 568 Nature 336, 336-343 (2019).

[632] *Id.*

to declare brain death. However, the possibility of restoring cell function indicates towards false brain death diagnoses.[633] Some scholars argue that certain level of brain functions was preserved in Jahi McMath's case and highlights the limitations of the existing clinical standards.[634][635]

Recently, the Nevada Supreme Court considered a case[636] which reflected the disorientation between the statutory language used by UDDA and the accepted clinical standards. Ms. Hailu, a young college student slipped into a coma after she underwent a surgery. She was placed on life-support, however, did not show brainstem reflexes for over a month. Her physicians performed the apnea and other ancillary tests, which led them to the conclusion that she was brain dead. Her father sued against this declaration. During the trial, the hospital cited that their tests aligned with the American Academy of Neurology (AAN) guidelines and those were the accepted clinical standards in the state. However, Dr. Byrne and Dr. Callister (who are strong opponents of brain death) gave testimonies to support her father's claims. They questioned the validity and reliability of the guidelines as they did not assess all functions of the brain.[637] However, the trial court approved the certification of brain

---

[633] *See supra note* 622.

[634] *See supra note* 628.

[635] *See supra note* 626.

[636] Gabreyes v. Prime Healthcare Services. (In re Estate of Hailu), 361 P.3d 524 (Nev. 2015).

[637] *Id.*

death. Her father appealed to the Supreme Court of Nevada. The Supreme Court found that the trial court's order can only be upheld if the clinical standards adopted by the hospital are "accepted medical standards" among other states who have adopted UDDA.[638] The evidence presented by the hospital was a report of the New Jersey Law Revision Commission that talked about the AAN guidelines, however, the hospital failed to identify that the Commission had actually disagreed with the guidelines. Thus, the Supreme Court remanded the case back to the trial court as it could not find that the medical community in general accepted the AAN guidelines and the statutory language of the Nevada's Determination of Death Act.[639] The case couldn't go further because Ms. Hailu passed away due to a cardiopulmonary arrest.[640]

Another issue is that of the lack of public trust in healthcare and the concept of brain death. Marginalized communities tend to be skeptical about the concept of brain death due to the lack of trust in the healthcare system that constantly disregards their pain and ailments.[641][642] Many people tend to develop opinions on brain death

---

[638] *Id.*

[639] Nev. Rev. Stat. § 451.007(1)(b) (2015).

[640] Siobhan McAndrew, *The Contested Death of Aden Hailu*, RENO GAZETTE-J (Mar. 25, 2016), http://www.rgj.com/story/news/2016/03/25/contested-death-aden-hailu/.

[641] Michele Goodwin, *Revisiting Death: Implicit Bias and the Case if Jahi McMath*, 48 Hastings Cent Rep S77, S77-S80 (2018).

[642] Katharina M.B., What Does the Public Need to Know About Brain Death? 12 AMA J Ethics e1047, e1048 (2020).

based on erroneous representations propagated by conservative media.[643] A recent study found that a high level of misinformation exists in the articles and news published about brain death in the United States.[644] The most common misinformation is the rejection of the scientific validity of the concept. For instance, terms like the 'Hand of God' or 'miracle' is used to describe incidents where supposedly brain-dead patients woke up from coma.[645][646] These articles fail to identify that brain-dead people never wake up because they are dead, and that these are mere instances of false diagnoses.

Another form of misinformation is the misconceived dichotomy between brain death and legal death. Media seldom acknowledges that brain death is legal death.[647][648]These wrong representations make the public believe that brain

[643] *Id.*

[644] Lewis A., Lord A.S., et al., Public Education and Misinformation on Brain Death in Mainstream Media 30 Clin Transplant 1082, 1082-1089 (2016).

[645] Finney D., *Hand of God Wakes Brain-Injured Girl from Coma*, USA TODAY (May 13, 2015), https://www.usatoday.com/story/news/nation/2015/05/13/hand-of-god-heals-iowa-girl/27274399.

[646] Newscore, Husband Celebrates Miracle as Brain Dead Wife Wakes Up in Hospital, FOX NEWS (May 11, 2011), https://www.foxnews.com/health/husband-celebrates-miracle-as-brain-dead-wife-wakes-up-in-hospital.

[647] St. John W., *The Irish Patient and Dr. Lawsuit*, N.Y. TIMES (Apr. 24, 2005), https://www.nytimes.com/2005/04/24/fashion/sundaystyles/the-irish-patient-and-dr-lawsuit.html.

[648] Galofaro C., *Mom Loses Battle to Keep Brain-Dead Baby on Life Support*, USA TODAY (Jul. 23, 2014), https://www.usatoday.com/story/news/nation/2014/07/23/baby-brain-dead/13042475/.

death is equivalent to coma, and not legal death.[649] This misinformation also perpetuates the notion that withdrawing life support from brain-dead patients aims at making organ transplantation trade convenient and liability-free.[650][651]

To resolve these issues, the first step would be to acknowledge that the concept of brain death may be interpreted differently by people owing to their socio-cultural upbringing, political ideologies, and religious beliefs. When human body is intrinsically political[652], it should not be a surprise that brain death too shall remain political.[653] Governments need to devise comprehensive policies to generate awareness about the scientific reasoning behind brain death determination.[654] In order to do that, we must first dismantle misinformation and conspiracies being spread about the concept. This can be done through education[655], laws to develop

---

[649] Siminoff L.A., Burant C., et al., *Death and Organ Procurement: Public Beliefs and Attitudes*, 59 Soc Sci Med. 2325, 2325-2334 (2004).

[650] *See supra note* 214.

[651] Joffe A.R., *The Ethics of Donation and Transplantation: Are Definitions of Death Being Distorted for Organ Transplantation?*, 2 Philos Ethics Humanit Med. 28, 28 (2007).

[652] Nadia V., Sarah A.G., *Body Politics*, 5 Politics, Groups, and Identities 1, 1-3 (2016).

[653] Shewmon D.A., *Brain Death: A Conclusion in Search of a Justification*, 48 Hastings Cent Rep. S22, S22-S25 (2018).

[654] *See supra note* 644.

[655] *See supra note* 642.

media literacy[656][657], public engagement[658], and fixing ethical standards for professionals.[659] Some scholars have proposed an idea to treat brain death as a legal fiction.[660] But this is problematic as it develops a dichotomy between brain death and legal death, when the public is unaware that the legal fiction of brain death may not be compatible with the existing biological notions of death.[661] It may also lead to chaos and misinformation about brain death.[662]

Another common issue surrounds the exact moment of death. Identifying exactly when a person died is vital to several legal issues.[663] The clinical and legal standards of death must be aligned to determine the exact time of an individual's death. Even though most of the states adopted the UDDA, the language of their legislations varies in this regard. Judges must try to interpret the statutes focusing on the underlying objectives of the law,

---

[656] Amy H.J., Zoelle B.Z., et al., *Investigation of Public Perception of Brain Death Using the Internet*, 154 Chest 286, 287 (2018).

[657] Lewis A., Thaddeus M.P., *Why Should We See Brain Death as Socially Situated?*, 22 AMA J Ethics e983, e983-e985 (2020).

[658] Katina Z., Stephanie S., et al., *Public Understandings of the Definition and Determination of Death: A Scoping Review*, 8 Transplant Direct e1300, e1300 (2022).

[659] Gurpreet K., Joffe A.R., *The Intractable Problems with Brain Death and Possible Solutions*, 16 Philos Ethics Humanit Med. 107, 107-109 (2021).

[660] Shah S.K., Robert Truog, et al., Death and Legal Fictions 37 J Med Ethics 719, 719-722 (2011).

[661] *See supra note* 659.

[662] Robert Truog, Franklin Miller, *Changing the Conversation About Brain Death*, 14 A.J.O.B. 9, 9-14 (2014).

[663] Jason L. Goldsmith, *Wanted! Dead and/or Alive: Choosing Among the Not-So-Uniform Statutory Definitions of Death*, 61 U. Miami L. Rev. 871, 872 (2007).

rather than a plainly interpreting the meaning of the words.

State laws must include provisions that permit technological advancements to be used to review their own UDDAs.[664] The Federal Government can review the clinical standards during fixed intervals of time (say, annually, or every 2-5 years) and ensure that the law is aligned with the medical discoveries and innovations related to brain death determination. Idaho's law defines accepted clinical standards as the procedures used in the community where the decision is being made.[665] This is a problem because a person who is alive in one state may be then declared dead in another state.

The Federal Government can enact a statute that brings uniformity of brain death determination across the states. Congress is vested with the power to enact such a law.[666] However, the scope of this paper does not permit discussion of jurisdictional arguments. It is high time that we realize that the time of death should not be a subjective decision made by the judges.[667] The determination of death must be uniform, and this can be only done by a federal law.[668] Another aspect to popularize brain

---

[664] Haw. Rev. Stat. Ann. § 327C-1(e) (2016).

[665] Idaho Code § 54-1819 (2016).

[666] *See supra note* 32.

[667] *See* generally, e.g., In re Haymer, 450 N.E.2d 940; In re Schmidt's Estate. 261 Cal. App.2d 262 (1968).

[668] Ben Nipper, *Legislating Death: A Review and Proposed Refinement of the Uniform Determination of Death Act*, 17 Hous. J. Health L. & Pol'y 429, 435 (2017).

death is to clarify the diagnostic criteria and prevent possibilities of false diagnoses. This can be done by acknowledging the existing mismatch between law and clinical practices[669][670], strengthening and revising the testing standards[671], and amending the UDDA.[672][673]

---

[669] *See supra note* 247.
[670] *See supra note* 625.
[671] Marco de L.E., et al., *The Observation Period After Clinical Brain Death Diagnosis According to Ancillary Tests: Differences Between Supratentorial and Infratentorial Brain Injury*, 266 Neurol 1859, 1860-1868 (2019).
[672] Robert Truog, *Defining Death-Making Sense of the Case of Jahi McMath*, 319 JAMA 1859, 1859-1860 (2018).
[673] Miller F.G., Robert Truog, *The Incoherence of Determining Death by Neurological Criteria: A Commentary on Controversies in the Determination of Death: A White Paper by the President's Council on Bioethics* 19 Kennedy Inst Ethics J. 185, 185-193 (2009).

CHAPTER 11

SETTING OUT A MODEL LAW FOR INDIA

As evident from the previous sections, there is a dire need to create a comprehensive legal framework to govern the determination of brain death in India. It should outline the procedure to determine brain death, the constitution of the medical committee empowered to declare brain death, the relevant certificates or documents acceptable for all legal and administrative purposes, and the exceptions under which brain death may not be declared. So, the initial step would be to amend THOTA or introduce a new legislation. It may be challenging to introduce a new legislation given the current socio-political circumstances and the upcoming parliament elections in India.

If the government were to amend THOTA to include specific provisions about brain death, the procedure would be cumbersome. The procedure to amend a national legislation is lengthy. As per Article 368[674] of the Indian Constitution, a bill to amend a law passed by the Parliament must be passed both houses with a majority and must be ratified by at least half of the state legislatures. The

[674] *See supra note* 471. Part XX.

Union Government is highly likely to be reluctant to touch such a volatile subject that may spark debates amongst various conservative religious groups. However, what the government can do now is to introduce national guidelines to unify the procedure of determination of brain death.

It is vital to analyze how the Union Government derives the power to issue binding national guidelines. Article 73[675] defines and delimits the executive powers of the Union Government.[676] This power extends to the subjects that can be legislated by the Parliament.[677] The Union Government may issue guidelines, directions, or orders to the states in matters which are dealt with by the Parliament, according to a decision made by the Supreme Court of India in accordance with Article 73.[678] However, it does not authorize the Union Government to command states in matters exclusively within the domain of the state governments as it would amount to the violation of the separation of powers doctrine.[679]

Article 256[680] empowers the Union Government to ensure state compliance with Union laws (equivalent to federal law). The Union Government

[675] *Id.* Part V.

[676] A. Kotaiah Naidu v. State of Andhra Pradesh (Writ Petition No. 322 of 1958) (Ind.).

[677] State of Andhra Pradesh v. P. Laxmi Devi & Others (Writ Petition No. 12649 of 2000) (Ind.).

[678] State of Rajasthan v. Union of India, 1984 SCC (2) 292 (Ind.).

[679] State of West Bengal v. Union of India, 1964 SCR (1) 371 (Ind.).

[680] *See supra note* 674. Part XI.

can issue directions under this executive power to instruct state(s) to perform what is necessary to achieve specific goals. Since THOTA falls under the Union list, the Union Government has the authority to issue national guidelines in this regard. More specifically, the Ministry of Health and Family Welfare will have the power to issue guidelines related to brain death as it is responsible to implement THOTA and oversee the organ transplantation in India.[681]

In the turbulent times through which we are passing, an analysis of the Indian philosophical tradition is much more than a matter of antiquarian curiosity. Without this inevitable inquiry, we may remain helpless pawns in the grim political game undertaken to misrepresent the quintessence of Indian wisdom. Indian renaissance has reiterated that any thoughts that are not founded upon secularism, rationalism, and scientific knowledge form the deadweight of the past that impedes the nation's progress. Hence, it is high time that we discard the unethical approach that dismantles the actual intention of the organ transplant legislations.

Disclaimer: The researcher attempts to draft some model guidelines rooted in the core principles of bioethics that can be adopted by the Union Government. The guidelines have been derived by analyzing the Standard Operating Procedure of

---

681 NATIONAL ORGAN & TISSUE TRANSPLANT ORGANIZATION, https://notto.mohfw.gov.in/ (last visited Jun. 1, 2023).

Kerala and other relevant international standards. The guidelines are grounded in scientific reasoning and logic. It is to be noted that these guidelines may also be converted into a comprehensive legislation if the Union Government decides to regulate the determination of brain death through a statute.

National Model Guidelines for the Standard Determination of Brain Death

Provision 1: Purpose

The National Guidelines for the Standard Determination of Brain Death in India seeks to establish uniform and standard practices and protocols to determine brain death across the country. These guidelines seek to ensure the accurate diagnosis of brain death while promoting ethical and legal standards in organ transplantation and end-of-life care.

Provision 2: Definition of Brain Death

Brain Death is the irreversible cessation of all cerebral and brainstem functions, including consciousness, brainstem reflexes, and spontaneous respiration, and it is distinguishable from other states like coma, vegetative state, or minimally conscious state. For all administrative and legal purposes, brain death shall be considered as death.

Provision 3: Informed Consent

Brain Death can only be certified after obtaining the informed consent of the family members or the surrogate decision-maker of the patient. Transparent processes and simple documents must be used to obtain informed consent. The Annexure contains sample templates that can be used by the hospital to obtain informed consent. If there is sufficient evidence to indicate that the patient would have consented to the determination of brain death or the withdrawal of life support, her individual autonomy shall override the wishes of the family members.

Provision 3: Diagnosis of Brain Death

(a) The patient must be in an irreversible coma.

(b) Reversible causes like hypothermia, intoxication, neuromuscular blockade, and severe metabolic derangement must be excluded.

(c) A neurologist or neurosurgeon must conduct thorough neurological examinations to assess the absence of cerebral and brainstem function, including cranial nerve reflexes, motor responses, and brainstem reflexes.

(d) Thereafter, an apnea test must be performed to confirm the absence of respiratory drive.

(e) If doubt persists, it is highly recommended that the medical professionals perform confirmatory tests including EEG and cerebral angiography.

If a nominal majority of the medical panel raises doubts, these ancillary tests must be mandatorily performed.

(f) An appropriate time interval, typically, 6 hours, should pass between the initial and confirmatory tests, to ensure careful observation and documentation.

(g) If the patient remains unresponsive after the second round of apnea test and other ancillary tests, she shall be declared brain dead.

(h) All the findings, examinations, and tests must be meticulously documented, including the timing of initial and confirmatory tests.

(i) All the tests must be mandatorily observed by all the members of the medical panel.

(j) If the clinical findings are unreliable, the medical panel may abandon the certification process.

Provision 4: Medical Panel

The medical panel shall have the authority to certify brain death. A registered medical practitioner who is the general administrator of the hospital, the registered medical practitioner who treats the patient, a neurosurgeon or neurologist, and a registered medical practitioner from the committee instituted by the State Government, shall form the panel. The State Government shall have the power to form a committee of registered medical practitioners who act independently on the medical panel. This shall ensure impartiality of the decision.

Provision 5: Certification of Brain Death

At least two registered medical practitioners including the neurosurgeon or neurologist must certify brain death. This certificate shall be a comprehensive proof of death and shall be used for all legal and administrative purposes. This certificate shall be deemed equivalent to the death certificate issued under the Registration of Births and Deaths Act.

Annexure:

Informed Consent Template (to be issued on the official letter head of the hospital and addressed to the family member or the surrogate decision-maker)

Informed Consent for the Determination of Brain Death: We understand that (Patient's Name) is currently admitted to our hospital. We are writing to seek your informed consent for the determination of brain death as an essential step in the medical evaluation process.

Explanation of Brain Death: Brain death determination confirms that there is no chance of recovery and establishes the legal and medical basis for the end-of-life decisions, including withdrawal of life-sustaining treatments, and organ transplants. To determine brain death, a comprehensive evaluation shall be performed by the medical panel and involves a series of clinical examinations and tests to assess the complete loss of brain function. These tests are performed under stringent medical and ethical protocols. There are no additional risks involved. This determination aims to facilitating informed decision-making related to the nature, type, and extent of the treatment.

Alternatives: In case brain death is not established, alternative treatment options can be explored, and this shall be discussed with you by the medical panel.

Voluntary Consent: Your consent for brain death determination is completely voluntary. You have the right to refuse or withdraw consent at any point of the process. Your decision shall not affect the quality of care.

Confidentiality and Privacy: All medical information and data related to the patient shall be treated with strict confidentiality. The process shall be carried out in compliance with the applicable privacy laws. More information related to the privacy protection shall be made available upon request.

This form must be signed by both the surrogate decision-maker and the registered medical practitioner who handles the general administration of the hospital. The rationale of involving this particular medical practitioner is to highlight the utmost care and importance given to the process.

CHAPTER 12

CONCLUSION: SUMMARIZED ETHICAL ANALYSIS

The researcher finds that brain death is legal death, and that it is a legally, ethically, and morally justifiable standard of death in human beings. Brain death is legal death in the United States; however, the position is still unclear in India due to lack of a coherent legislation. The concept of brain death is widely accepted across the world through adherence to bioethical principles and the enactment of specific statutes related to death. Brain death is a scientifically sound concept and an objective criterion of legal death.

Brain death has been established through legislations, case laws, and consensus of the medical community. Brain death indicates the irreversible nature of loss of brain function and reflexes. Whenever the patient has issued an advanced directive or the appointed a surrogate decision maker to make her end-of-life decisions, those choices are given the utmost value.[682] This upholds individual autonomy.[683] Medical professionals understand the emotional and ethical implications of the declaration of brain death, and they generally

[682] *See supra* note 674.
[683] Gonzales v. Oregon, 546 U.S. 243 (2006).

act according to the principle of beneficence. Brain death determination is made based on a measurable, objective criteria ratified by statutes and case laws. This ensures a just and fair assessment of the condition of the patient.

Opponents of brain death argue that brain death determination was developed for merely meeting the utilitarian needs of the organ transplant enterprise. They argue that such determination diminishes the opportunity for recovery and limits the quality of the treatment. However, brain death has received widespread consensus due to its scientific validity that ensures evidence-based decisions. Another argument is that the determination of brain death leads to improper withdrawal of life support. This argument falls short because withdrawal of life-sustaining treatments cannot be done without strict adherence to law and clinical protocols. Physicians may be held liable for assault or even murder if they do not abide by the clinical guidelines to make the determination. This ensures that the patient's best interests always triumph. This also avoids any harm that may be caused to the patient.

Some critics argue that brain death is against certain religious beliefs, however, brain death is a medical truth, rather than a subjective issue. For instance, several Catholic scholars have vehemently opposed brain death determination and subsequent organ transplants in the recent past, but the Vatican has always considered organ donation as a morally and ethically acceptable act of charity. Religious notions may vary about brain death, but several states have started considering the possibility of including a provision to place conscientious objection against brain death determination in their death laws. Another concern is about how brain death determination may adversely affect marginalized populations who do not have an equal footing in clinical decisions, compared to their privileged counter parts. But case laws and ethical standards require that brain death determination can only be done by following the principles of justice and equity, and there are several strong laws against discrimination.

Brain death facilitates proper organ transplants that may save millions of lives across the globe. It is in accordance with the principle of maximum benefits for the public. It restricts futile treatments, reducing harm to the dead individual, and permits optimal allocation of resources within hospitals. This is in accordance with the principles of distributive justice and equity. Brain death determination shall never be made if the patient expressed interests against such determination, which upholds the right to self-determination.[684] Brain death criteria have been developed to ensure a just, fair, and objective standard to determine death.

Determination of brain death represents the best interests of the patient[685] as it seeks to bring

[684] Moore v. Regents of the University of California, 51 Cal. 3d 120 (1990).
[685] In re Quinlan, 355 A.2d 647 (1976).

clarity in end-of-life decisions and several legal interests. It upholds the dignity of the patient. The determination weighs the benefits of continuing life support against respecting the right to die with dignity. It thoroughly examines any potential for improvement, and brain death is only declared when there is ample clinical evidence to prove that there is no chance for recovery. Thus, the determination involves the ethical balancing[686] of quality and quantity of life. Before declaring brain death, the physicians consider various factors including the rights of the patient and surrogate decision maker(s) and the potential impact on the limited resources within the healthcare setting.

The ethical guidelines issued by various medical professional organizations attempts to ensure trust in the shared decision making. This ensures that the medical decision is in alignment with the principles of beneficence and nonmaleficence. Finally, brain death determination is only made in adherence to the legal precedents and relevant statutes, and the right to privacy and informed consent.

---

[686] Bouvia v. Superior Court, 179 Cal. App. 3d 1127, 1138-1139 (1986).

BIBLIOGRAPHY

1. 210 ILL. COMP. STAT. 85/6.23 (2012).
2. A COMPREHENSIVE HISTORY OF INDIA – PART 3 (P.N. Chopra & M.N. Das et. al. eds., 2003).
3. *A Definition of Irreversible Coma: Report of the Ad Hoc Committee of the Harvard Medical School to Examine the Definition of Brain Death,* JAMA., 205, 337-340 (1968).
4. *A.B.A: The Voice of the Profession – Annual Report 1980-81,* 67 A.B.A.J. 1479 (1981) (explaining the intent of UDDA to reduce uncertainty in this crucial medical-legal arena).
5. Aasled R. et al., *Noninvasive Transcranial Doppler Ultrasound Recording of Flow Velocity in Basal Cerebral Arteries,* 57 J. Neurosurg. 769-774 (1982).
6. Abbasi P., Nouri P., et al., *The Obstacles to Organ Donation Following Brain Death in Iran: A Qualitative Study,* 21 BMC Med. Ethics 83, 83 (2020).
7. Abdelmalek C., Goyal S., et al., *Advance Directives: Give Teeth to End-of-Life Choices,* 6 Aging Well 24, 24-27 (2013).

8. Abdul Al-Hashim, Mujahid Al-Busaidi, *Understanding the Concept of Brain Death in the Middle East*, 30 OMJ 75, 75-76 (2015).

9. Aboubakr M. et al., *Brain Death Criteria*, NIH (Nov. 27, 2022, 9:00 AM), https://www.ncbi.nlm.nih.gov/books/NBK545144/

10. Act No. 18/1969 (Ind.).

11. Act No. 42/1994 (Ind.).

12. Act No. 45/1860 (Ind.).

13. Adam Kovac, *Inside the Heated Scientific Debate to Redefine Who is Dead*, THE DAILY BEAST (Jul. 6, 2022, 2:42 PM), https://www.thedailybeast.com/inside-the-heated-scientific-debate-to-redefine-who-is-dead.

14. Adam, Omelianchuk, Art, Caplan, et al., *Revise the UDDA to Align the Law with Practice through Neurorespiratory Criteria*, 98 Neurol. 532, 532-536 (2022).

15. Adewole Adamson, Avery Smith, *Machine Learning and Healthcare Disparities in Dermatology*, 154 JAMA Dermatol 1247, 1248 (2018).

16. *Advance Directives and Surrogate Decision Making*, CENTER FOR HEALTH ETHICS, (Jul. 3, 2023, 10:11 AM), https://medicine.missouri.edu/centers-institutes-labs/health-ethics/faq/advance-directives.

17. Agnew S., *The Meaning and Significance of Conscience in Private Law*, 77 C.L.J. 479, 479-505 (2018).

18. Akira Akayabashi, *Japanese Parliament Passes Brain-Death Law*, 349 LANCET 1895, 1895 (1997).

19. Alanna Vial, David Stirling, et al., *The Role of Deep Learning and Radiomic Feature Extraction in Cancer-Specific Predictive Modelling: A Review*, 7 Transl Cancer Res 803, 803-816 (2018).

20. Alberto G., Savulescu J., *Beyond Money: Conscientious Objection in Medicine as a Conflict of Interests*, 17 J Bioeth Inq. 229, 229-243 (2020).

21. Alexander Capron, Leon Kass, *A Statutory Definition of the Standards for Determining Human Death: An Appraisal and a Proposal*, 121 U. PENN. L. REV. 87 (1972) (they drafted a model law wherein death could be assessed using the brain death criteria only under circumstances where artificial means of support preclude a determination that spontaneous and respiratory and circulatory functions have ceased; but this model law was also ambiguous).

22. Alexandra S., *Virtue Ethics and Its Potential as the Leading Moral Theory*, 12 Discussions 1, 1-2 (2015).

23. Alyson S., *Issues with the Determination of Brain Death: The Case for Religious and Moral Exceptions*, Law School Student Scholarship 1106 (2020).

24. *AMA Insights,* 243 JAMA, 419, 420 (1980).

25. American Academy of Pediatrics, *Clinical Report: Guidelines for the Determination of Brain Death in Infants and Children: An Update of the 1987 Task Force Recommendations,* 128 PEDIATRICS e720 (2011).

26. Amit Kaushal, Russ Altman, et al., Geographic Distribution of U.S. Cohorts Used to Train Deep Learning Algorithms, 324 JAMA 1212, 1213 (2020).

27. Amy Cheng, *The Pigs Had Been Dead for an Hour: Scientists Made Their Hearts Beat Again,* THE WASH. POST, (Aug. 4, 2022, 05:22 AM), https://www.washingtonpost.com/science/2022/08/04/yale-organex-dead-pigs-revived/.

28. Amy H.J., Zoelle B.Z., et al., *Investigation of Public Perception of Brain Death Using the Internet,* 154 Chest 286, 287 (2018).

29. AN APPRAISAL OF THE CRITERIA OF CEREBRAL DEATH: A SUMMARY STATEMENT, JAMA (1977).

30. Anamika Krishnan, *UDBHR: An Interpretation in the Indian Medico-Legal and Bioethical Context,* 214, 227 in BIOETHICS OF THE CRAZY APE (Oguz Kelemen, Gergely Tari ed., 2019).

31. Anderson J.K., *A Biblical Appraisal of Euthanasia,* in LIVING ETHICALLY IN THE 90s 198-201 (Anderson J.K. ed., 1990).

32. Anne L., et al., *Family Members' Requests to Extend Physiologic Support After Declaration of Brain Death: A Case Series Analysis and Proposed Guidelines for Clinical Management,* 25 J. CLIN ETHICS, 222 (2014).

33. Anu Saini, *Physicians of Ancient India* 5 J Family Med. Prim. Care 254, 255-256 (2016).

34. Arlene's Flowers v. State of Washington, 138 S. Ct. 2671 (2018) (mem.).

35. Arthur L. Caplan et al., *Revise the Uniform Determination of Death Act to Align the Law with Practice Through Neurorespiratory Criteria,* 98 Neurol. 532-536 (2022) (discussing the advantages of neurorespiratory criteria to determine death).

36. *Artificial Intelligence/Machine Learning-Based Software as a Medical Device Action Plan,* FDA, https://www.fda.gov/media/145022/download.

37. Arvind Venkat, Julianna Becker, *The Effect of Statutory Limitations on the Authority of Substitute Decision Makers on the Care of Patients in the Intensive Care Unit: Case Examples and Review of State Laws Affecting Withdrawing or Withholding Life-Sustaining Treatment,* 29 J Intensive Care Med. 71, 71-80 (2014).

38. Astrup J., Symon L., et al., *Thresholds in Cerebral Ischemia: The Ischemic Penumbra,* 12 Stroke 723, 723-725 (1981).

39. Aziz Rahman, Mohsin Ali, et. al., *The British Art of Colonialism in India: Subjugation and Division,* 25 J. Peace Confl. Stud. 2, 7-8 (2018) (discussing the introduction of a British-styled curriculum in India and its failure).

40. Balajee K.L., Ramachandran N., et al., *Awareness and Attitudes Toward Organ Donation in Rural Puducherry, India,* 6 Ann Med Health Sci Res 286, 287-289 (2016).

41. Bandhua Mukti Morcha v. Union of India & Ors. (1997) 10 SCC 549; State of Punjab & Ors. v. Mohinder Singh Chawla, AIR 1997 SC 1225 (Ind.).

42. Baron L., Shemie S.D., et al., *Brief Review: History, Concept and Controversies in the Neurological Determination of Death,* 53 Can J Anaesth., 602, 602-608 (2006).

43. Basavarajegowda A., Arjunan C., et al., *A Comparative Study of Knowledge, Attitude, and Practices About Organ Donation Among Blood Donors and Non-Blood Donors,* 15 Asian J Transfus Sci 56 (2021).

44. Basil Varkey, *Principles of Clinical Ethics and Their Application to Practice,* 30 Med Princ Pract 17, 17-28 (2021).

45. Bedir A., Aksoy S., *Brain Death Revisited: It is not 'Complete Death' according to Islamic Sources,* 37 J. Med. Ethics 290, 294 (2011).

46. Ben Nipper, *Legislating Death: A Review and Proposed Refinement of the Uniform Determination of Death Act*, 17 Hous. J. Health L. & Pol'y 429, 435 (2017).

47. Benjamin Best, *Scientific Justification of Cryonics Practice*, 11 Rejuvenation Res. 493, 494 (2008).

48. Bernat J.L., *Controversies in Defining and Determining Death in Critical Care*, 9 Nat Rev Neurol 164, 164-173 (2013).

49. Bernat J.L., *On Irreversibility as a Prerequisite for Brain Death Determination*, 550 Adv. Exp Med Biol. 161, 161-167 (2004).

50. Bernat J.L., *On Noncongruence Between the Concept and Determination of Death*, 43 Hastings Cent Rep 25, 25-33 (2013).

51. Bharambe V.K. HR M., et al, *Awareness Regarding Body and Organ Donation Amongst the Population of an Urban City in India*, 5 J Health allied Sci NU 51, 51-57 (2015).

52. Bianca Miller, *Nurses in the Know: The History and Future of Advance Directives*, 22 OJIN 57, 57 (2017).

53. Bigon, L., Njoh, A.J., *Power and Social Control in Settler and Exploitation Colonies: The Experience of New France and French Colonial Africa*, 53 JAAS 932, 935 (2018).

54. Bjorn K., Morten M., *Conscientious Objection to Intentional Killing: An Argument for Toleration*, 19 BMC Med Ethics 82, 82-83 (2018).

55. BLACK'S LAW DICTIONARY (11th ed. 2019).

56. Bouvia v. Superior Court, 179 Cal. App. 3d 1127, 1138-1139 (1986).

57. BRAIN DEATH, THE DETERMINATION OF BRAIN DEATH, AND MEMBER GUIDANCE FOR BRAIN DEATH ACCOMODATION REQUESTS: AAN POSITION STATEMENT, AMERICAN ACADEMY FOR NEUROLOGY (2019).

58. BRITANNICA, https://www.britannica.com (last visited Dec. 11, 2022).

59. Brittany M. Lee, et al., *Can a Parent Refuse the Brain Death Examination?*, 145 Pediatric 2340, 2345 (2020).

60. Britzer P. Vincent, Gurch Randhawa et al., *Barriers Towards Deceased Organ Donation among Indians Living Globally: An Integrative Systematic Review Using Narrative Synthesis*, 12 BMJ 1-18 (2022).

61. Brophy v. New England Sinai Hospital, Inc., 497 N.E.2d 626 (Mass. 1986).

62. Brown v. United States, 890 F.2d 1329, 1347 (5th Cir. 1989).

63. Bryan Neihart, *What is Freedom of Conscience, and Why Does it Matter?* ALLIANCE DEFENDING FREEDOM, (Apr. 11, 2023), https://adflegal.org/article/what-freedom-conscience-and-why-does-it-matter.

64. Burkle C.M., Sharp R.R., et al., *Why Brain Death is Considered Death and Why There Should be No Confusion,* 83 Neurol., 1464, 1469 (2014).

65. Burwell v. Hobby Lobby Stores Inc., 573 U.S. 682 (2014).

66. Byrne P.A., et al., *Brain Death is False,* 66 Linacre 42, 48 (1999).

67. Byrne P.A., et al., *Brain Death: An Opposing Viewpoint,* 242 JAMA 71, 71-80 (1979).

68. C. Whitehead, *The Historiography of British Education Policy, Part 1: India,* 34 Hist. Educ. 300, 315-329 (2005).

69. C.K. NAMBOODIRI, VISHAVAIDYASARAMUCHAYA (1st ed. 2006) (this is a treatise on toxicology with special reference to the physicians in the State of Kerala).

70. CAL. HEALTH & SAFETY CODE § 1254.4 (a) 2012.

71. Calixto Machado et al., *Brain Death Diagnosis and Apnea Test Safety,* 12 Ann Indian Acad Neurol., 197-200 (2009).

72. Calixto Machado et al., The Concept of Brain Death did not Evolve to Benefit Organ Transplants, 33 J Med Ethics., 197-200 (2007).

73. Caplan, A., Magnus, David, *Brain Death is Really Death,* TIME (Jan. 3, 2014, 5:45 AM), https://time.com/194/brain-death-really-is-death/.

74. Card R., *Reasonability and Conscientious Objection,* 28 Bioethics 320, 320-326 (2014).

75. Carla Bleiker, *OrganEx Tells Cells Not to Die,* DW (Aug. 3, 2022), https://www.dw.com/en/organex-may-save-donor-organs-by-telling-cells-not-to-die/a-62697834.

76. Carnival Leisure Indus v. Aubin, 53 F.3d 716, 719 (5th Cir. 1995).

77. CAROLINE ELKINS, LEGACY OF VIOLENCE: A HISTORY OF THE BRITISH EMPIRE 12 (2022).

78. Chaim, Dovid Z., *Accommodating Religious Objections to Brain Death: Legal Considerations,* 17 JHCS 49, 64-65 (1989).

79. Chandler C., Foltz P., et al., *Using Machine Learning in Psychiatry: The Need to Establish a Framework that Nurture Trustworthiness,* 46 Schizophr Bull 11, 11-14 (2020).

80. CHARAKA SAMHITA (V.J. Trikamji ed. 2014) (this is considered to be the most authentic reference to Ayurveda).

81. Chris P. McKay, *What is Life and How Do We Search for It in Other Worlds?*, 2(9) PLoS Biol. 1261, 1260-1263 (2004) (discussing comparable patterns in the organics of life on earth and space).

82. Church of Lukumi Babalu Aye v. City of Hialeah, 508 U.S. 520 (1993).

83. Clark E., *Healthcare Decision Making and Declarations in New York,* wings.buffalo.edu/faculty/research/bioethics/case.html. (2004).

84. Claude Hemphill, *Do Not Resuscitate Orders, Unintended Consequences, and the Ripple Effects,* 11 Crit Care 121, 121 (2007).

85. Claudio Cohen, Bioethicists Must Rethink the Concept of Death: *The Idea of Brain Death is not Appropriate for Cryopreservation,* 67 Clinics Sao Paulo 93, 93-94 (2012).

86. Clay v. United States, 403 U.S. 698 (1971).

87. Cohen A., Nirenberg A., *Current Practices in Advance Care Planning: Implications for Oncology Nurses,* 15 CJON 547, 547-553 (2011).

88. Coimbra C.G., *Implications of Ischemic Penumbra for the Diagnosis of Brain Death* 32 Braz J Med Biol Res. 1479, 1479-1487 (1999).

89. Coimbra, C.G., *Implications of Ischemic Penumbra for the Diagnosis of Brain Death,* 32 Braz J. Med Biol Res 1479, 1479-1487 (1999).

90. Commonwealth v. Golston, 366 N.E.2d 744 (1977).

91. Cowley C., *A Defense of Conscientious Objection in Medicine: A Reply to Schuklenk and Savulescu,* 30 Bioethics 358, 358-364 (2016).

92. *Criteria for the Diagnosis of Brainstem Death,* 29 J R Coll. Physicians Lond. 381-382 (1995).

93. *Criteria for the Diagnosis of Brainstem Death,* 29 J R Coll. Physicians Lond. 381-382 (1995).

94. Cruzan v. Director, Mo. Dept. of Health, 497 U.S. 261 (1990).

95. Cynthia J., *Conscientious Objection, Not Refusal: The Power of a Word,* 88 Linacre Q., 242, 242-246 (2021).

96. D Alan Shewmon, *Statement in Support of Revising the Uniform Determination of Death Act and in Opposition to a Proposed Revision,* J. Med Philos., jhab014 (2021).

97. D. ARNOLD, COLONIZING THE BODY: STATE MEDICINE AND EPIDEMIC DISEASE IN NINETEENTH CENTURY INDIA (1st ed. 1993).

98. D. ARNOLD, SCIENCE, TECHNOLOGY AND MEDICINE IN COLONIAL INDIA (1st ed. 2000).

99. D.M. Shaner et al., Really, *Most SINCERELY Dead: Policy and Procedure in the Diagnosis of*

Death by Neurologic Criteria, 62 Neurol. 1683 (2004).

100. Dalle Ave A.L., Bernat J.L., *Inconsistences Between the Criterion and Tests for Brain Death,* 35 J Intensive Care Med 772, 772-780 (2020).

101. Damini Sharma, Amrish Chandra, *Medical Device Rules – 2017, India: An Insight,* 7 Appl. Clin. Res. Clin. Trials Regul. Aff. 126, 126-134 (2020).

102. Daniel Payne, *U.S. Bishops Warn Against Proposed Change to Definition of Death,* CAN (Jul. 20, 2023, 09:12 AM), https://www.ncregister.com/cna/u-s-bishops-warn-against-proposed-change-to-definition-of-brain-death.

103. Daniel Sperling, *Should a Patient who is Pregnant and Brain Dead Receive Life Support, Despite Objection from Her Appointed Surrogate?,* 22 AMA J Ethics e1004, e1005 (2020).

104. Daniele S.G., Silbereis J., et al., *Restoration of Brain Circulation and Cellular Functions Hours Post-Mortem,* 568 Nature 336, 336-343 (2019).

105. David Albert Jones, *The UK Definition of Death,* 140 LAW & Just. – Christian L. REV. 56, 57 (1999).

106. David Forster, *When the Body is Soul: The Proposed Japanese Bill on Organ Transplantations from Brain Dead Donors,* 3 PAC. RIM L.& POL'Y J. 103, 105 (1994).

107. David Shaw, Dale Gardiner, et al., *Family over Rules? An Ethical Analysis of Allowing Families to Overrule Donation Intentions,* 101 Transplant. 482, 482-487 (2017).

108. David Skrbina, *Plato and the Meaning of Life,* in THE MEANING OF LIFE AND THE GREAT PHILOSOPHERS 8 (Stephen Leach ed., 2018).

109. DAVID W. DEAMER & GAIL R. FLEISCHAKER, ORIGINS OF LIFE: THE CENTRAL CONCEPTS (1994) (summarizing the suggestion of Carl Sagan to redefine life in the cosmos).

110. DeJohn P., *New CMS Guidelines Suggest Changes in Advance Directive Policies,* 29 OR Manager 1,1 (2013).

111. DETERMINATION OF DEATH ACT, https://www.uniformlaws.org/committees/community-home?CommunityKey=155faf5d-03c2-4027-99ba-ee4c99019d6c (last visited Jan. 27, 2023).

112. Dhanwate, D. Anant, *Brainstem Death: A Comprehensive Review in the Indian Perspective,* 18 IJCCM, 596, 597 (2014).

113. *Diagnosis of Brain Death: Statement issued by the Honorary Secretary of the Conference of Medical Royal Colleges and their Faculties in the United Kingdom on 11 October 1976,* 2 Br. Med J. 1187, 1187-1188 (1976).

114. *Diagnosis of Brain Death: Statement issued by the Honorary Secretary of the Conference of Medical Royal Colleges and their Faculties in the United Kingdom on 11 October 1976*, 2 Br. Med J. 1187, 1187-1188 (1976).

115. *Diagnosis of Death: Memorandum issued by the Honorary Secretary of the Conference of Medical Royal Colleges and their Faculties in the United Kingdom on 15 January 1979*, 2 Br. Med J. 332 (1979).

116. Dianne L. Atkins, Stuart Berger, et al., *Pediatric Life Support and Cardiopulmonary Resuscitation Quality: 2015 American Heart Association Guidelines Update for CPR and Emergency Cardiovascular Care*, 132 Circ. J. 519, 525 (2015).

117. DIRK MODES & DAN STONE, COLONIALISM AND GENOCIDE 7 (2007).

118. Donald Kollisch, Robert Santulli, et al., *The Limits of Advance Directives in Maintaining Autonomy in Patients with Advanced Dementia*, 134 Am J Med 963, 963-967 (2021).

119. DONALD MCRAE, EVERY SECOND COUNTS: THE RACE TO TRANSPLANT THE FIRST HUMAN HEART 4 (2006).

120. Donald Redelmeier, Damon Scales, *Missing the Diagnosis of Brain Death as a Self-Erasing Error*, 192 Am J Respir Crit Care Med 280, 280-282 (2015).

121. Donaldson T.M., *Ethical Resources for the Clinician: Principles, Values and Other Theories,* in CONTEMPORARY ISSUES IN BIOETHICS 15-38 (Beauchamp ed., 2003).

122. Doug McConnell, *Conscientious Objection in Healthcare: Pinning Down the Reasonability View,* 46 J Med Philos. 37, 37-47 (2021).

123. Douglas v. Janssen Funeral Homes, No. 2KB-09-173CI, 2010 WL 9069780, 6-7 (Alaska Super. Ct., Nov. 19, 2010).

124. Dr. S. Ganapathy v. State of Kerala, WP(C) No. 5552 of 2017, High Court of Kerala. (Ind.)

125. Dunning D., Johnson K., et al., *Why People Fail to Recognize Their own Incompetence,* 12 Curr Dir Pyschol Sci 83, 83-87 (2003).

126. Ed Lavandera, *Texas Judge: Remove Brain-Dead Woman from Ventilator, Other Machines,* CNN HEALTH (Jan. 24, 2014, 10:09 PM), https://www.cnn.com/2014/01/24/health/pregnant-brain-dead-woman-texas/.

127. EDGAR ALLAN POE, POETRY AND TALES: THE PREMATURE BURIAL (Patrick F. Quinn ed., Library of America 1984) (1844).

128. Eelco Wijdicks, Brain Death, 118 Handb. Clin. Neurol. 191, 191-203 (2013).

129. Eichner v. Dillon, 52 N.Y.S.2d 517, 533 (1980).

130. Eileen Baker, Catherine Marco, *Advance Directives in the Emergency Department,* 1 J Am Coll Emerg Physicians Open. 270, 270-275 (2020).

131. Elise Reuter, *5 Takeaways from the FDA's List of AI-enabled Medical Devices,* MED TECH DIVE (Nov. 7, 2022, 09:30 AM), https://www.medtechdive.com/news/FDA-AI-ML-medical-devices-5-takeaways/635908/.

132. Elise Reuter, *Software to Predict Risk of Sepsis, Stroke Should be Regulated as a Medical Device,* Says FDA, MED TECH DIVE (Oct. 11, 2022, 10:12 AM), https://www.medtechdive.com/news/fda-regulate-sepsis-software/633732/.

133. Employment Division v. Smith, 494 U.S. 872 (1990).

134. Erick Munoz v. John Peter Smith Hospital (Cause No. 096-270080-14) (2014).

135. Erika Chamberlain, *McKitty v. Hayani: Time for Canada to Clarify its Legal Definition of Death,* 14 MCGILL J.L. & HEALTH 219, 224 (2021).

136. Erin Barnes, et al., *Inconsistency in Brain Death Determination Should not be Tolerated,* 22 AMA J Ethics e1027, e1027-e1032 (2020).

137. Estol C.J., *To Live and Let Die: A Brain Death Symposium at the Pontifical Academy of Science,* 2(3) Int. J Stroke. 227, 227-229 (2007) (discussing

the modern Christian view articulated by Pope Benedict XVI).

138. Eva Winkler, *Do Researchers in Empirical Ethics Studies Have a Duty to Act Upon their Findings? Case Study in End-of-Life Decision Making,* 14 J Empir Res Hum Res Ethics 438, 438-439 (2019).

139. Evers J.C., et al., *Brain Death: Still a Controversy,* 53 The Pharos of Alpha Omega Alpha 10, 10-12 (1990).

140. *FDA Launches the Digital Health Center of Excellence,* FDA News Release (Sep. 22, 2020) https://www.fda.gov/news-events/press-announcements/fda-launches-digital-health-center-excellence.

141. Field, D.R., et al., *Maternal Brain Death During Pregnancy: medical and Ethical Issues,* 260 JAMA 816, 862 (1988).

142. Finney D., *Hand of God Wakes Brain-Injured Girl from Coma,* USA TODAY (May 13, 2015), https://www.usatoday.com/story/news/nation/2015/05/13/hand-of-god-heals-iowa-girl/27274399.

143. Forest Simon, *Pig Cells Restored Through Death-Defying OrganEx Technology,* GENENG NEWS, (Aug. 4, 2022), https://www.genengnews.com/news/pig-cells-restored-through-death-defying-organex-technology/.

144. Fred Rosner, *The Definition of Death in Jewish Law,* in THE DEFINITION OF DEATH: CONTEMPORARY CONTROVERSIES 210-215 (Stuart Youngner et al. ed., 1999).

145. Fred Shapiro, *Quotes Uncovered: Death and Taxes,* FREAKONOMICS (Feb. 12, 2011, 1:30 PM), http://freakonomics.com/2011/02/17/quotes-uncovered-death-and-taxes/.

146. FRIEDRICH WILHELM NIETZSCHE, THUS SPOKE ZARATHUSTRA: A BOOK FOR ALL AND NONE (Walter Kaufmann trans., Modern Library 1995) (1883).

147. Fulton v. City of Philadelphia, 320 F. Supp. 3d 661 (2021).

148. Gabbay E., Fins J., *Go in Peace: Brain Death, Reasonable Accommodation and Jewish Mourning Rituals,* 58 J. Relig. Health 1672, 1679 (2019).

149. Gabreyes v. Prime Healthcare Services. (In re Estate of Hailu), 361 P.3d 524 (Nev. 2015).

150. Gabriel B., Pope T., et al., *Reason-giving and Medical Futility: Contrasting Legal and Social Discourse in the United States with the United Kingdom and Ontario, Canada,* 150 CHEST J. 714, 716 (2016).

151. Gail A., Van Norman, *A Matter of Life and Death: What Every Anesthesiologist Should Know about the Medical, Legal, and Ethical Aspects of Declaring Brain Death,* 91 Anesthesiol 275, 275-277 (1999).

152. Gallups v. Cotter, 534 So.2d 585 (Ala. 1988); Lovato v. District Court, 601 P.2d 1072 (Colo. 1979); Dority v. Superior Court, 145 Cal. App.3d 273 (Cal. App. 1983).

153. Galofaro C., *Mom Loses Battle to Keep Brain-Dead Baby on Life Support,* USA TODAY (Jul. 23, 2014), https://www.usatoday.com/story/news/nation/2014/07/23/baby-brain-dead/13042475/.

154. Gareth J., *The Problematic Symmetry Between Brain Birth and Brain Death,* 24 J Med Ethics 237, 237-242 (1998).

155. George S., Thomas M., et al., *Somatic Survival and Organ Donation among Brain-dead patients in the State of Qatar,* 16 Neurol., 207, 207-208 (2016).

156. Gidey Amare, *Reviewing the Values of a Standard Operating Procedure,* 22 Ethip J Health Sci. 205, 205-208 (2012).

157. Gonzales v. Oregon, 546 U.S. 243 (2006).

158. Goodwin, Michele, *Implicit Bias and the Case of Jahi McMath,* 48 Hastings Cent. Rep., S77, S77-S78 (2018).

159. Gopendra C. Kamal, Sourav Ballav et. al., *Evolution of Diagnostic Techniques of Death: Ayurveda Perspective and Modern Trends in India,* 6 IJRG 109, 110 (2018).

160. Gorelick, R.E., *Apartheid and Colonialism,* 19 CILSA 70, 70-71 (1986).

161. Goudreau J.L., et al., *Complications during Apnea Testing in the Determination of Brain Death: Predisposing Factors,* 55 Neurol. 1045, 1048 (2000).

162. GOVERNMENT OF SINGAPORE: WHAT IS HOTA ALL ABOUT? (2013) https://www.gov.sg/article/what-is-hota-all-about.

163. GOVINDA PARAYIL, KERALA: THE DEVELOPMENT EXPERIENCE (1st ed. 2000).

164. Greer D.M., Robinson J.D., et al., *Variability of Brain Death Policies in the United States,* 73 Neurol 213, 214 (2016).

165. Greer, D.M., Shemie S.D., et al., *Determination of Brain Death/Death by Neurologic Criteria: The World Brain Death Project,* 324 JAMA 1078, 1081 (2010).

166. Greitz T. et al., *Aortocranial and Carotid Angiography in Determination of Brain Death,* 5 Neurorad. 13-19 (1973).

167. Griswold v. Connecticut, 381 U.S. 479 (1965).

168. *Guidelines for the determination of death. Report of the medical consultants on the diagnosis of death to the President's Commission for the Study of Ethical Problems in Medicine and Biomedical and Behavioral Research,* 246 JAMA 2184-6 (1981).

169. Gurpreet K., Joffe A.R., *The Intractable Problems with Brain Death and Possible Solutions,* 16 Philos Ethics Humanit Med. 107, 107-109 (2021).

170. Guthrie, *Brain Death and Criminal Liability,* 15 CRIM. L. BULL. 40, 42 (1979).

171. H. Lammer et al., *What Makes a Planet Habitable?,* 17(2) Astron. Astrophys Rev. 181-249 (2009) (discussing the connection of life to habitability).

172. H. Richard Beresford, *Book Review,* 27 N.Y.L. SCH. L.R. U.L.A. 593, 17, 30-31 (1982).

173. H.L. Hirsh, *Brain Death,* 21 MED. TRIAL TECH Q. 377, 378-379 (1975) (concluding that human beings die in stages, proceeding through clinical death to brain death, to biological death, and ultimately cellular death).

174. H.L.A. HART, THE CONCEPT OF LAW (2nd ed. 1994).

175. Halevy A & Broody B, *Brain Death: Reconciling Definitions, Criteria, and Tests,* 119 Ann Intern Med. 519-525 (1993).

176. Hammad S., Fawzi M., et al., *Questionnaire on Brain Death and Organ Procurement,* 15 Exp. Clin Transplant 121, 121-123 (2017).

177. HARPER LEE, GO SET A WATCHMAN (2015).

178. HARPER LEE, TO KILL A MOCKINGBIRD (1960).

179. Harris Funeral Homes v. EEOC, 590 U.S. __ (2020).

180. Harsh Deora, Nishant Yagnick, *The Legal Void Outside Brain Death in India: The Legislative Need of DNR in Brain Death,* 71 Neurol India 20, 20-27 (2023).

181. Hasan S., *The Challenges of Conscientious Objection in Healthcare,* 55 J Relig Health 384, 384-393 (2016).

182. Haw. Rev. Stat. Ann. § 327C-1(e) (2016).

183. Hayden Field, *IBM Takes Another Shot at Watson as A.I. Boom Picks Up Steam,* CNBC NEWS (May 9, 2023, 06:00 AM), https://www.cnbc.com/2023/05/09/ibm-takes-another-shot-at-watson-as-ai-boom-picks-up-steam.html.

184. HEALTH AND FAMILY WELFARE DEPARTMENT, GOVERNMENT OF KERALA, STANDARD OPERATING PROCEDURE FOR BRAIN DEATH CERTIFICATION IN GOVERNMENT AND PRIVATE HOSPITALS IN THE STATE (2018) https://www.knos.org.in/pdf/53-2018-BRAIN%20DEATH-SOP.pdf.

185. Helene Caux, *Effects of Colonialism Still being Felt to this Day,* U.N. NEWS (Feb. 18, 2022), https://news.un.org/en/story/2022/02/1112292.

186. Ho Chi Minh, *The Path that Led Me to Leninism,* in DECOLONIZATION 47-49 (Raymond F. Betts ed., 2004).

187. Hoffenberg R., *Christiaan Barnard: His First Transplants and Their Impact on Concepts of Death,* 323 BMJ 1478, 1479 (2001).

188. https://www.usccb.org/resources/Joint_submission_NCBC_and_USCCB_on_UDDA_2023.pdf.

189. Hughes J.R., *Limitations of the EEG in Coma and Brain Death,* 315 Ann. NY Acad Sci. 121-136 (1978).

190. Human Organ and Tissue Donation Act, SNS 2010, Section 2(j) (Can.).

191. Hussain A., Malik A., et al., *The Use of Robotics in Surgery: A Review,* 68 Int J Clin Pract. 1376, 1376-1382 (2014).

192. Ian Austen, *Brain-Dead: A Canadian Woman Remains a Silent Partner Awaiting Birth,* THE N.Y. TIMES (Feb. 6, 2014, 6:45 PM), https://www.nytimes.com/2014/02/07/world/americas/brain-dead-a-canadian-woman-lives-on-as-a-silent-partner-awaiting-birth.html.

193. Ian Keith McDaniel, Life and Death Issues in Bioethics: Abortion, Persistent Vegetative State, and the Definition of Death (Dec. 4, 2015) (Ph.D. dissertation, University of Kansas) (on file with author).

194. Idaho Code § 54-1819 (2016).

195. IMMANUEL KANT, CRITIQUE OF JUDGMENT (1st ed. 1987).

196. IMMANUEL KANT, CRITIQUE OF PRACTICAL REASON (Lewis White Beck trans., The Bobbs-Merrill 1956) (1788).

197. In re Allen Callaway, no. DG-16-08 (Pondera County Dist. Ct., Mont. 2016).

198. In re Guardianship of Hailu, 361 P.3d 524 (Nev. 2015)

199. In re Haymer, 115 III. App.3d 349 (1983).

200. In re Haymer, 450 N.E.2d 940; In re Schmidt's Estate. 261 Cal. App.2d 262 (1968).

201. In re Lawson v. VCU Medical Center, No. CL16-2358 (2016).

202. In re Mirranda Grace Lawson, no. CL16-2358 (City of Richmond Circuit Court, Va. 2016).

203. In re Quinlan, 355 A.2d 647 (1976).

204. In re Storar, 52 N.Y.2d 363 (1981).

205. In re The Guardianship of A.C., No. DE-16-08 (2016).

206. In re UH (Ont. CCB Oct 28, 2016); In re EI (Ont. CCB Sep. 30, 2016) (Can.).

207. In re Welfare of Bowman, 94 Wash.2d 407 (1980).

208. International Covenant on Civil and Political Rights, Dec. 16, 1966, 999 U.N.T.S. 171, art. 18 § 1.

209. International Covenant on Civil and Political Rights, Dec. 16, 1966, 999 U.N.T.S. 171, art. 18 § 1.

210. Inwald D, Jakobovits I, Petros A., Brain Stem Death: *Managing Care When Accepted Medical Guidelines and Religious Beliefs are in Conflict: Consideration and Compromise are Possible,* 320 BMJ 1266, 1266-1267 (2000).

211. Irving S. Wright, *Who Should Make the Decisions?* in THE MOMENT OF DEATH 3, 4 (Arthur Winter ed., 1969) (discussing traditional criteria for determination of death).

212. Ishmael Bradley, *Conscientious Objection in Medicine: A Moral Dilemma,* CLINICAL CORRELATIONS, (May. 28, 2009), https://www.clinicalcorrelations.org/2009/05/28/conscientious-objection-in-medicine-a-moral-dilemma/.

213. J.A. Anderson et al., *Refusal of Brain Death Diagnosis: The Health Lawyer's Perspective,* 9 JONAS HEALTH CARE L. ETHICS & REG. 90 (2007).

214. Jack Clark, *Artificial Intelligence has a Sea of Dudes Problem,* BLOOMBERG TERMINAL, (Jun. 27, 2016), https://www.bloomberg.com/professional/blog/artificial-intelligence-sea-dudes-problem/.

215. Janani Sampath, *Kerala Shows Way With SOPs for Brain Death Certification,* THE FEDERAL,

(Feb. 15, 2020, 7:10 AM), https://thefederal.com/health/kerala-shows-way-with-standard-operating-procedure-for-brain-death-certification/.

216. Jason L. Goldsmith, *Wanted! Dead and/or Alive: Choosing Among the Not-So-Uniform Statutory Definitions of Death,* 61 U. Miami L. Rev. 871, 872 (2007).

217. Jason Wells, *Jahi McMath is Brain Dead; Hopes for Life are Futile: Experts Say,* LA TIMES (Dec. 13, 2013, 12:00 PM), https://www.latimes.com/local/lanow/la-xpm-2013-dec-30-la-me-ln-jahi-mcmath-case-misconceptions-20131230-story.html.

218. Jennifer Bertkau, Lori Herbst, *Ethics of Pediatric and Young Adult Medical Decision-Making: Case-Based Discussions Exploring Consent, Capacity, and Surrogate Decision Making,* 17 MedEdPORTAL 11094, 11094 (2021).

219. JEREMY BENTHAM, AN INTRODUCTION TO THE PRINCIPLES OF MORALS AND LEGISLATION (1st ed. 1823).

220. Jessa Boubker, Nathan Beaver, et al., *FDA's New Guidance Proposes Flexible Use of AI in Medical Devices,* FOLEY (May 10, 2023), https://www.foley.com/en/insights/publications/2023/05/fdas-guidance-flexible-use-ai-medical-devices.

221. Joel Achenbach, *Scientists Restore Some Brain Cell Functions in Pigs Four Hours After Death,*

THE WASH. POST, (Apr. 17, 2019, 1:00 PM), https://www.washingtonpost.com/science/2019/04/17/scientists-restore-some-brain-cell-functions-pigs-four-hours-after-death/.

222. Joffe A.R., *The Ethics of Donation and Transplantation: Are Definitions of Death Being Distorted for Organ Transplantation?*, 2 Philos Ethics Humanit Med. 28, 28 (2007).

223. Joffe, A.R., Carcillo, J., et al., *Donation After Cardiocirculatory Death: A Call for a Moratorium Pending Full Public Disclosure and Fully Informed Consent*, 6 Philos Ethics Humanit Med 17 (2011).

224. John H. Matheson, *Conscientious Objection to Military Service*, THE FIRST AMENDMENT ENCYCLOPEDIA, (Jan. 23, 2009), https://www.mtsu.edu/first-amendment/article/912/conscientious-objection-to-military-service.

225. John Henry Newman, *Conscience Quotes*, NOTABLE QUOTES, http://www.notable-quotes.com/c/conscience_quotes.html.

226. John Lizza, *Why DCD Donors are Dead*, 45 J Med Philos 42, 42-45 (2020).

227. JOHN WITTE JR. & JOEL A. NICHOLS, RELIGION AND THE AMERICAN CONSTITUTIONAL EXPERIMENT, (3rd ed. 2011).

228. Johnson v. Rodriguez, 943 F.2d 104, 110 (1st Cir. 1991).

229. Johnson, L.S., *The Case for Reasonable Accommodation of Conscientious Objections to Declarations of Brain Death,* 13 Bio. Inq. 105, 105-115 (2016).

230. JOINT COMMITTEE ON BIOMEDICAL ETHICS OF THE LOS ANGELES COUNTY MEDICAL ASSOCIATION & LOS ANGELES COUNTY BAR ASSOCIATION, GUIDELINES FOR PHYSICIANS: FORGOING LIFE-SUSTAINING TREATMENT FOR ADULT PATIENTS (2006).

231. Jos Chathukulam, Joseph Tharamangalam, *The Kerala Model in the Time of COVID-19: Rethinking State, Society and Democracy,* 137 World Dev. 105207 (2021).

232. Joshi M.S., *Whose Decision Is It? Organ Donation Attitudes Among Young UK South Asians,* 56 Psychol Stud, 86, 86-97 (2011).

233. Julie McCarthy, *Fasting to the Death: Is it a Religious Rite or Suicide?* NPR (Sep. 2, 2015, 5:20 AM), https://www.npr.org/sections/goatsandsoda/2015/09/02/436820789/fasting-to-the-death-is-it-a-religious-rite-or-suicide.

234. K. LOCHAN, MEDICINES OF EARLY INDIA 90 (1st ed. 2003).

235. K. MAHADEVASASTRIKAL, VISHA VAIDYA JYOTSNIKA: AN ENGLISH TRANSLATION (3rd ed. 1958).

236. Kantymir L., McLeod C., *Justification for Conscience Exemptions in Healthcare,* 28 Bioethics, 16, 16-23 (2014).

237. Kartikeyan Sundaram, *India's Population Has Already Overtaken China's, Analysts Estimate,* BLOOMBERG (Jan. 17, 2023, 11:49 PM), https://www.bloomberg.com/news/articles/2023-01-18/india-s-population-overtakes-china-to-become-world-s-biggest-analysts-estimate?leadSource=uverify%20wall.

238. Kartina A. Choong, M.Y. Rady et. al., *Re A (A Child) and the United Kingdom Code of Practice for the Diagnosis and Confirmation of Death: Should a Secular Construct of Death Override Religious Values in a Pluralistic Society?* 30 HEC Forum. 71, 71-89 (2018) (comparing the secular construct in U.K. to the UDDA in U.S.A.).

239. Kate Crawford, *Artificial Intelligence's White Guy Problem,* N.Y. TIMES, (Jun. 25, 2016, 10:11 AM), https://www.nytimes.com/2016/06/26/opinion/sunday/artificial-intelligences-white-guy-problem.html.

240. Katharina M.B., What Does the Public Need to Know About Brain Death? 12 AMA J Ethics e1047, e1048 (2020).

241. Katie Hunt, *Researchers Revive Cells in Pig Organs Hour After Animal's Death: What This Could Mean for Humans?* ABC NEWS, (Aug. 4, 2022), https://abc7ny.com/yale-dead-pigs-pig-research-organex-brought-back-to-life/12097812/.

242. Katina Z., Stephanie S., et al., *Public Understandings of the Definition and Determination of Death: A Scoping Review,* 8 Transplant Direct e1300, e1300 (2022).

243. Ken Holmes, *Buddhism and Death,* KAGYU SAMYE LING BLOG (Jan. 3, 2023, 3:41 AM), https://www.samyeling.org/buddhism-and-meditation/teaching-archive-2/dharmacharya-ken-holmes/buddhism-and-death/.

244. Kerr Estate v. BC Motorist Insurance Co. [1972] 6 WWR 400 (BCSC); Johannisse v. Johannisse Estate [1985] OJ No. 1273 (QL) (H Ct J) (Can.).

245. Khan F.A., *The Definition of Death in Islam: Can Brain Death be Used as a Criteria of Death in Islam?,* 18 JAMA. 18, 18-21 (1986) (discussing the absence of a precise definition of departure of soul in Quran).

246. Kim, S.J., et al., *Persistent Stunning Induces Myocardial Hibernation and Protection – Flow/Function and Metabolic Mechanisms,* 92 Circ Res 1233 (2003).

247. Kirsten Rabe Smolensky, *Defining Life from the Perspective of Death: An Introduction to the Forced Symmetry Approach,* 41 U Chi Legal. 44, 41-86

(2006) (suggesting a symmetric understanding of life and death).

248. Konkel, Lindsay, *The Brain Before Birth: Using fMRI to Explore the Secrets of Fetal Neurodevelopment,* 126 E.P.H. 1,2 (2018).

A. Kotaiah Naidu v. State of Andhra Pradesh (Writ Petition No. 322 of 1958) (Ind.).

249. Kristin Walter, *Brain Death,* 324 JAMA 1116 (2020).

250. Kulkarni S., Reddy N. et al., *Facial Expression (Mood) Recognition from Facial Images using Committee Neural Networks,* 8 Biomed Eng. Online 16, 16 (2009).

251. Kushner T., *Having a Life Versus Being Alive,* 10 J Med Ethics 5, 5-8 (1984).

252. Lakshmi Kumar, *Brain Death and Care of the Organ Donor* 32 J Anaesthesiol Clin Pharmacol 146, 146-152 (2016).

253. Larry Celegans, *OrganEx Team Revives Dead Pig's Organs: Implications for Cryonics,* LONGEVITY (Aug. 12, 2022), https://www.longevitydao.net/blog-posts/reviving-pigs-cryonics.

254. Laurie Clarke, *Why the Sci-Fi Dream of Cryonics Never Died,* MIT TECHNOLOGY REVIEW, (Oct. 24, 2022), https://www.technologyreview.com/2022/10/14/1060951/cryonics-sci-fi-freezing-bodies/.

255. Leclerc (Succession) v. Turmel [2005] RJQ 1165 (SC) (Can.).

256. Letter from the National Catholic Bioethics Center to the Uniform Determination of Death Committee of the Uniform Law Commission (Jul. 12, 2023)

257. Lewis A., Adams N., et al., *Organ Support after Death by Neurologic Criteria: Results of a Survey of U.S. Neurologists,* 87 Neurol. 827, 827-834 (2016).

258. Lewis A., Adams N., et al., *Organ Support after Death by Neurologic Criteria in Pediatric Patients,* 45 Crit Care Med e916, e916-e925 (2017).

259. Lewis A., Bonnie R.J., et al., *It is Time to Revise the Uniform Determination of Death Act,* 172 Ann Intern med 143, 144 (2020).

260. Lewis A., Lord A.S., et al., Public Education and Misinformation on Brain Death in Mainstream Media 30 Clin Transplant 1082, 1082-1089 (2016).

261. Lewis A., Thaddeus M.P., *Why Should We See Brain Death as Socially Situated?,* 22 AMA J Ethics e983, e983-e985 (2020).

262. Lewis, A., Blosser, S., et al., *An Interdisciplinary Response to Contemporary Concerns about Brain Death Determination,* 90 Neurol. 423, 423-426 (2018).

263. Liberman A., *Wrongness, Responsibility and Conscientious Refusal in Healthcare*, 31 Bioethics 495, 495-504 (2017).

264. Little Sisters of the Poor v. Pennsylvania, 591 U.S. __ (2020).

265. LON L. FULLER, THE MORALITY OF LAW (1964).

266. Los Angeles Times Staff, *Jahi McMath: Expert Criticizes keeping Girl on Ventilator*, LA TIMES (Jan. 13, 2014, 12:00 PM), https://www.latimes.com/local/lanow/la-xpm-2014-jan-13-la-me-ln-jahi-mcmath-ventilator-20140113-story.html.

267. Lovato v. District Court In and For Tenth Judicial Dist., 198 Colo. 419, 425 (1979).

268. Lucy Grindon, *Possible Brain Death Law Changes Pose Ethical Concerns*, NATIONAL CATHOLIC REPORTER (May 11, 2021, 2:00 PM), https://www.ncronline.org/news/possible-brain-death-law-changes-pose-ethical-concerns.

269. Lukas J.M., *The Demise of Brain Death*, 73 BJPS 487, 491 (2022).

270. M.A. Alam, *Imperialism and Science*, 4 Soc. Scien. 3, 6-15 (1977) (discussing the attempts to smother local scientific knowledge).

271. M.J. Clarke et al., *Beyond Transplantation: Considering Brain Death As a Hard Clinical Endpoint*, 14 AM. J. BIOETHICS 43, 43-45 (2014).

272. M.J. Newton, *Precedent Autonomy: Life-Sustaining Intervention and the Demented Patient,* 8 Camb Q Healthc Ethics 189, 189-199 (1999).

273. M.V. PYLEE, INDIA'S CONSTITUTION 3, (5th ed. 1994).

274. Machado C., Kerein J., et al., *The Concept of Brain Death did not Evolve to Benefit Organ Transplants,* 33 J Med. Ethics 197, 197-200 (2007).

275. Mahika Ahluwalia, *Legal Governance of Brain Data Derived from Artificial Intelligence,* 7 Voices in Bioethics 1, 1-3 (2021).

276. Manas Manu, Gaurav Anand, *A Review of Medical Device Regulations in India, Comparison with European Union and Way-Ahead,* 13 Perspect Clin Res. 3, 3-4 (2022).

277. Maneka Gandhi v. Union of India, AIR 1978 SC 597 (Ind.).

278. Marco de L.E., et al., *The Observation Period After Clinical Brain Death Diagnosis According to Ancillary Tests: Differences Between Supratentorial and Infratentorial Brain Injury,* 266 Neurol 1859, 1860-1868 (2019).

279. Maria Jose Valero, *Freedom of Conscience of Healthcare Professionals and Conscientious Objection in the European Court of Human Rights,* 13 Religions 558, 558 (2022).

280. *Marketing Submission Recommendations for a Predetermined Change Control Plan for Artificial*

Intelligence/Machine Learning- Enabled Device Software Functions, FDA (Apr. 2023), https://www.fda.gov/regulatory-information/search-fda-guidance-documents/marketing-submission-recommendations-predetermined-change-control-plan-artificial.

281. Martin S. Pernick, *Brain Death in a Cultural Context: The Reconstruction of Death,* in *supra* note 17.

282. Masterpiece Cakeshop v. Colorado Civil Rights Commission, 370 P.3d 272 (2018).

283. McKitty v. Hayani, 2019 ONCA 805 (Can.).

284. Medical Devices (Amendment) Rules, 2020 (Ind.) https://cdsco.gov.in/opencms/opencms/en/Medical-Device-Diagnostics/Medical-Device-Diagnostics/.

285. MERRIAM WEBSTER DICTIONARY (12th ed. 2022)

286. Michael A. Lev, *Amid a Need for Organ Donors, Japan Debates Brain Death: Two Bills Challenge Spiritual Belief,* CHICAGO TRIBUNE, Apr. 15, 1997, at 5.

287. Michael Nair-Collins, et al., *Hypothalamic-Pituitary Function in Brain Death,* 31 J Intensive Care Med 41, 41-45 (2016).

288. Michele Buenafe, *The FDA Regulatory Landscape for AI in Medical Devices,* MED DEVICE ONLINE (Mar. 3, 2023), https://www.meddeviceonline.

com/doc/the-fda-regulatory-landscape-for-ai-in-medical-devices-0001.

289. Michele Goodwin, *Revisiting Death: Implicit Bias and the Case if Jahi McMath,* 48 Hastings Cent Rep S77, S77-S80 (2018).

290. Michelle Garcia-Olp, *How Colonization Impacts Identity through the Generations: A Closer Look at Historical Trauma and Education* (Aug. 1, 2018) (Ph.D. dissertation, University of Denver) (on file with author).

291. Milan Sharma, Gulam Jeelani, *India's Organ Crisis Deepens,* INDIA TODAY (Jan. 05, 2020, 02:29 AM), https://www.indiatoday.in/mail-today/story/india-s-organ-crisis-deepens-1634029-2020-01-04.

292. Miller F.G., Robert Truog, *The Incoherence of Determining Death by Neurological Criteria: A Commentary on Controversies in the Determination of Death: A White Paper by the President's Council on Bioethics* 19 Kennedy Inst Ethics J. 185, 185-193 (2009).

293. Mishra P.R., Mohakud S., et al., *A Comparison Between Medical and Non-Medical Students in India for Cadaveric Organ Donation,* 33 J Fore Med Toxicol 5, 5-12 (2016).

294. Mohandas, A. et al., *A Clinical and Pathological Study,* 35 J Neurosurg. 211, 211-218 (1971).

295. Mollaret P. & Goulon M., *Le Coma Depasse*, 101 Rev. Neurol. 3, 15 (1959).

296. Moore v. Regents of the University of California, 51 Cal. 3d 120 (1990).

297. Mughis Sheerani, Mian Urfy et. al., *Brain Death: Concepts and Knowledge amongst Health Professionals in Province of Sindh, Pakistan*, 58 JPMA 352, 354-355 (2008).

298. Myers C., Woods R., *Conscientious Objection? Yes, But Make Sure It is Genuine*, 7 AJOB 19, 19-20 (2007).

299. N.J. REV. STAT. § 26:6A-5; N.J. ADMIN. CODE § 13:35-6A.6.

300. Nadia V., Sarah A.G., *Body Politics*, 5 Politics, Groups, and Identities 1, 1-3 (2016).

301. NAFTALI MOSES, REALLY DEAD? THE ISRAELI BRAIN-DEATH CONTROVERSY 1967-1986 (1st ed. 2011).

302. Nair-Collins, M., Miller, F.G., *Do the Brain Dead Merely Appear to be Alive?* 43 J Med. Ethics 747, 751 (2017).

303. Nancy B., *Conscience Clauses, Healthcare Providers, and Parents*, HASTINGS BLOG, (Jun. 30, 2023), https://www.thehastingscenter.org/briefingbook/conscience-clauses-health-care-providers-and-parents/.

304. Natalia Norori, Qiyang Hu, et al., *Addressing Bias in Big Data and AI for Healthcare: A Call for Open Science*, 2 PATTERNS NY 100347 (2021).

305. Nathan G., Toni S., *A Taxonomy of Conscientious Objection in Healthcare*, 17 Clinical Ethics 63, 63-70 (2022).

306. Nathaniel M.R., James L.B., *What Should We Do About the Mismatch Between Legal Criteria for Death and How Brain Death is Diagnosed?*, 22 AMA J Ethics e1038, e1040 (2020).

307. NATIONAL HEALTH SERVICES, https://www.nhs.uk (last visited Dec. 24, 2022).

308. National Institute of Family and Life Advocates v. Becerra, 585 U.S. __ (2018).

309. NATIONAL ORGAN & TISSUE TRANSPLANT ORGANIZATION, https://notto.mohfw.gov.in/ (last visited Jun. 1, 2023).

310. Navtej Singh Johar v. Union of India, AIR 2018 SC 4321 (Ind.).

311. Nedilkjo Budisa, *Xenobiology: A Journey Towards Parallel Life Forms*, 21 ChemBioChem., 2229, 2228-2231 (2020).

312. Nev. Rev. Stat. § 451.007 (2017).

313. Nev. Rev. Stat. § 451.007(1)(b) (2015).

314. New York City Health & Hosp. Corp. v. Sulsona, 367 N.Y.S.2d 686, 689-90 (1975) (expert testimony signified that the kidneys obtained

from donors pronounced dead through the cardiopulmonary criteria were more prone to post-operative failure).

315. Newscore, Husband Celebrates Miracle as Brain Dead Wife Wakes Up in Hospital, FOX NEWS (May 11, 2011), https://www.foxnews.com/health/husband-celebrates-miracle-as-brain-dead-wife-wakes-up-in-hospital.

316. Nicholas Tonti-Filippini, *You Only Die Twice: Augustine, Aquinas, the Council of Vienne, and Death by the Brain Criterion,* 38 Communio 308, 308-325 (2011).

317. *No Longer Science Fiction, AI and Robotics are Transforming Healthcare,* PwC, (May. 30, 2023), https://www.pwc.com/gx/en/industries/healthcare/publications/ai-robotics-new-health/transforming-healthcare.html#:~:text=It%20puts%20consumers%20in%20control,and%20support%20for%20staying%20healthy.

318. Noble Gracious, Veena Roshan Jose, *Certification of Brain Stem Death in India: Medico-Legal Perspectives,* 16 Amrita J Med, 71, 71-76 (2020).

319. O'Reilly S., et al., *Brain Death: The Patient, the Physician, and Society,* 18 Gon Law Rev. 429, 429-516 (1982).

320. ORGAN TRANSPLANTATION: MEANINGS AND REALITIES 9, 13 (Stuart J. Younger et, al., eds., 1996).

321. *Organ Transplants Face Tough Going in Japan Despite Legislation, Cultural and Religious Beliefs Cause Obstacles,* ROCKY MOUNTAIN NEWS, Oct. 19, 1997, at 4.

322. Osamu Muramoto, *Informed Consent for the Diagnosis of Brain Death: A Conceptual Argument,* 11 Philos Ethics Humanit Med s13010, s13016 (2016).

323. Paige Carlson, *Pigs Escape Death by New Technology in Organ Revival,* PORK, (Aug. 4, 2022), https://www.porkbusiness.com/news/industry/pigs-escape-death-new-technology-organ-revival.

324. Pallis, C., *Whole Brain Death Reconsidered: Physiological Facts and Philosophy,* 9 J. Med Ethics 32, 35 (1983).

325. Papadatou D., Goldman A., et al., *The Team, in* TEXTBOOK OF INTERDISCIPLINARY PEDIATRIC PALLIATIVE CARE 55-63 (Wolfe J., ed. 2011).

326. Parmar, G., Lalani A.V., *The Sleeping Heart: Hibernating Myocardium,* 1 Pers. Cardio 44, 44-53 (2001).

327. Patrick Lee, German Grisez, *Total Brain Death: A Reply to Alan Shewmon,* 26 Bioethics 275, 275-284 (2010).

328. Paul A. Byrne, Walt F. Weaver, *Brain Death is not Death, in* BRAIN DEATH AND DISORDERS

OF CONSCIOUSNESS 43-44 (Machado and Shewmon ed., 2004).

329. PAUL M. TAYLOR, FREEDOM OF RELIGION, UN AND EUROPEAN HUMAN RIGHTS LAW AND PRACTICE (1st ed. 2005).

330. Paula Newton, *Brain-Dead Canadian Woman Dies after Son's Birth,* CNN HEALTH (Feb. 12, 2014, 7:32 AM), https://www.cnn.com/2014/02/11/health/canada-brain-dead-pregnant-woman/index.html.

331. Pellegrino E., *The Physician's Conscience, Conscience Clauses, and Religious Belief: A Catholic Perspective,* 30 Fordham Urban Law J 221, 221-244 (2002).

332. People v. Eulo, 63 N.Y.2d 341 (1984).

333. Pernick M.S., *Back from the Grave: Recurring Controversies Over Defining and Diagnosing Death in History,* in DEATH: BEYOND WHOLE-BRAIN CRITERIA 17-24 (Zaner R.M. ed., 1988) (discussing two essential questions in determining death; whether life can be limited to the functioning of one organ and how can we avoid the inaccurate diagnosis of death).

334. Peter Beaulieu, *When to Recommend a PEG Tube? A Decision Tree for Clinicians from a Catholic Perspective,* 79 Linacre Q. 25, 25-26 (2012).

335. Peter J., et al., *Organ Donation: Dead Donor Rule Sets Guidelines For Harvesting Organs*, 46 Opthal Times 1, 1-3 (2021).

336. PETER MCCULLAGH, BRAIN DEAD, BRAIN ABSENT, BRAIN DONORS: HUMAN SUBJECTS OR HUMAN OBJECTS? (1st ed. 1993).

337. Peter Simpson, David Bates et. al., *A Code of Practice for the Diagnosis and Confirmation of Death: 2008*, AMRC, https://www.aomrc.org.uk/reports-guidance/ukdec-reports-and-guidance/code-practice-diagnosis-confirmation-death/.

338. Peter Simpson, David Bates et. al., *A Code of Practice for the Diagnosis and Confirmation of Death: 2008*, AMRC, https://www.aomrc.org.uk/reports-guidance/ukdec-reports-and-guidance/code-practice-diagnosis-confirmation-death/.

339. PETER SINGER, RETHINKING LIFE AND DEATH: THE COLLAPSE OF OUR TRADITIONAL ETHICS 22 (1994).

340. Peter Singer, *The Challenge of Brain Death for the Sanctity of Life Ethic*, 8 Ethic & Bioethic 153, 158 (2018).

341. Phoebe Clark, Jayne Kim, et al., *Marketing and US Food and Drug Administration Clearance of Artificial Intelligence and Machine Learning Enabled Software in and as Medical Devices:*

A Systematic Review, 6 JAMA Netw Open e2321792 (2023).

342. Pope, Thaddeus, Bonnie, Richard J., et al., *It's Time to Revise the Uniform Determination of Death Act,* 172 Ann. Intern Med. 143, 143-144 (2020).

343. Poreddi V., Sunitha T.S., et al., *Gender Differences in Perceptions and Attitudes of General Population Towards Organ Donation: An Indian Perspective,* 28 Saudi J. Kidney Dis Transpl. 599 (2017).

344. Potts M., Evans D.W., *Does it Matter that Organ Donors are Not Dead? Ethical and Policy Implications,* 31 J Med Ethic 406, 406-407 (2005).

345. Prashanth Ram, Vikram Jain, *Living Will: Advance Medical Directive Enabling Dignity of Life in India,* THE IMPACT LAWYERS, (Jan. 14, 2021), https://theimpactlawyers.com/articles/living-will-advance-medical-directive-enabling-dignity-of-life-in-india.

346. PRESIDENT'S COMMISSION FOR THE STUDY OF ETHICAL PROBLEMS IN MEDICINE AND BIOMEDICAL AND BEHAVIORAL RESEARCH, DEFINING DEATH: MEDICAL, LEGAL AND ETHICAL ISSUES IN THE DETERMINATION OF DEATH (1981).

347. Press Trust of India, *At 96.2% Kerala Tops India's Literacy Rate Chart Again,* FIRSTPOST (Sep. 08, 2020, 13:37 PM), https://www.firstpost.com/india/at-96-2-kerala-tops-indias-literacy-rate-

chart-again-andhra-pradesh-ranks-lowest-with-66-4-8796401.html

348. *Proposed Regulatory Framework for Modifications to Artificial Intelligence/Machine Learning Based Software as a Medical Device: Discussion Paper,* FDA, https://www.fda.gov/media/122535/download.

349. *Proposed UDDA Revisions Expand law that Allows Euthanasia of Organ Donors,* ANGLICANS FOR LIFE, https://anglicansforlife.org/2023/05/31/proposed-udda-revisions-expand-law-that-allows-euthanasia-of-organ-donors/ (May 31, 2023).

350. R v. Green [1988] BCJ No. 1807 (BCSC) (Can.).

351. R v. Kitching and Adams [1976] 6 WWR 697 (MBCA) (Can.).

352. R v. Malcherek and R v. Steel, [1981] 1 WLR 690; Re A (A Minor) [1992] 3 Medical Law Reports 303 (Eng.).

353. R.D. Roy, *The Untold Story of Modern Science is One of Empire and Colonial Exploitation,* QUARTZ (Apr. 9, 2018, 6:56 AM), https://qz.com/india/1247577/the-untold-story-of-modern-science-is-one-of-empire-and-colonial-exploitation.

354. Rabbi Jason Weiner, *Death v. Brain Death in Judaism,* MY JEWISH LEARNING (Jan. 2, 2023,

6:56 AM), https://www.myjewishlearning.com/article/defining-death-in-jewish-law/

355. Rabbi Moshe D. Tendler, *Halakhic Death Means Brain Death,* 3 The Jew. Rev. 5750, 5751 (1990).

356. RABBINICAL COUNCIL OF AMERICA, HALACHIC ISSUES IN THE DETERMINATION OF DEATH AND IN ORGAN TRANSPLANTATION (2010).

357. Rachel Aviv, *What does it mean to Die?* THE NEW YORKER (Jan. 29, 2018, 10:03 AM), https://www.newyorker.com/magazine/2018/02/05/what-does-it-mean-to-die.

358. Rafael Domingo, *Restoring Freedom of Conscience,* 30 J.L. & Relig. 176, 176- 193 (2023).

359. Raiany Romanni, *Technology Promises to Change the Meaning of Death: At Least for Some,* THE WASH. POST, (Aug. 19, 2022, 10:19 AM), https://www.washingtonpost.com/outlook/2022/08/19/organex-yale-death-definition-medical-disparities/.

360. Range v. Douglas, 763 F.3d 573, 588 (6th Cir. 2014).

361. Re A (A Child) [2015] EWHC 443 (Fam) (Eng.).

362. Re A (A Minor) [1992] 3 Medical Law Reports 303 (Eng.).

363. Reynolds v. United States, 98 U.S. 145 (1879).

364. Rhiannon Williams, *Researchers Repaired Cells in Damaged Pig Organs an Hour after the Animal's Death,* MIT TECHNOLOGY REVIEW, (Aug. 3, 2022), https://www.technologyreview.com/2022/08/03/1056664/repair-cells-damaged-pig-organs-death-ethics-heart-brain/.

365. Richard Gibson, *The Ethics of OrganEx,* BMJ BLOG, (Aug. 12, 2022), https://blogs.bmj.com/medical-ethics/2022/08/12/the-ethics-of-organex/.

366. Ricki Lewis, *OrganEx Revives Pigs an Hour after Death, Holding Promise for Transplants,* PLOS BLOGS, (Aug. 4, 2022), https://dnascience.plos.org/2022/08/04/organex-revives-pigs-an-hour-after-death-holding-promise-for-transplants/.

367. Robert D. Truog, et al., *Counterpoint: Should Informed Consent be Required for Apnea Testing in Patients with Suspected Brain Death? Yes,* 152 Chest. 702, 702-704 (2017).

368. Robert D. Truog, *The Uncertain Future of the Determination of Brain Death,* 329 JAMA. 971, 971-972 (2023).

369. ROBERT M. VEATCH & LAINIE F. ROSS, DEFINING DEATH: THE CASE FOR CHOICE, 116 (1st ed. 2016).

370. Robert Orr, Autonomy, Conscience, and Professional Obligation, 15 Virtual Mentor 244, 244-248 (2013).

371. Robert Spaemann, *Is Brain Death the Death of a Human Person?* In LOVE AND THE DIGNITY OF HUMAN LIFE: ON NATURE AND NATURAL LAW 45-69 (Eerdmans, B., ed., 2012).

372. Robert Truog, *Death is Universal, But Sometimes Murky,* THE HARVARD GAZETTE, (Jul. 24, 2018), https://news.harvard.edu/gazette/story/2018/07/harvard-ethicist-robert-truog-on-why-brain-death-remains-controversial/.

373. Robert Truog, *Defining Death-Making Sense of the Case of Jahi McMath,* 319 JAMA 1859, 1859-1860 (2018).

374. Robert Truog, Franklin Miller, *Changing the Conversation About Brain Death,* 14 A.J.O.B. 9, 9-14 (2014).

375. Robert Truog, *Is it Time to Abandon Brain Death?,* 27 Hastings Cent Rep 29, 29-37 (1997).

376. Robert Truog, Robinson W.M., *Role of Brain Death and the Dead Donor Rule in the Ethics of Organ Transplantation,* 31 Crit Care Med 2391, 2391-2392 (2003).

377. RONALD DWARKIN, TAKING RIGHTS SERIOUSLY (1977).

378. Ronald M. Green, *Toward a Copernican Revolution in Our Thinking About Life's Beginning and Life's End,* 66 SOUNDINGS 152, 152-162 (1983)

(noting the significance of cell death: for every neuron which survives, six may die)

379. S.R. Bommai & Ors. v. Union of India & Ors. (1994) 3 SCC 1. (Ind.).

380. Safiye Celik, Scott M. Lundberg, *A Machine Learning Approach to Integrate Big Data for Precision Medicine in Acute Myeloid Leukemia*, 9 Nat Commun. 42, 42 (2018).

381. Sam D. Shemie et. al., *Severe Brain Injury to Neurological Determination of Death: Canadian Forum Recommendations*, 51 CMAJ 174 (2006).

382. Sarah Byers, *Life as Self Motion: Descartes and The Aristotelians on the Soul as the Life of the Body*, 59 Rev. Metaphys. 723-755 (2006).

383. Savulescu J., *Conscientious Objection in Medicine*, 332 BMJ 294, 294-297 (2006).

384. Savulescu J., Schuklenk U., *Doctors Have No Right to Refuse Medical Assistance in Dying, Abortion or Contraception*, 31 Bioethics, 162, 162-170 (2017).

385. Sawicki Nadia, *Disentangling Conscience Protections*, 48 Hastings Cent Rep 14, 14-22 (2018).

386. Schloendroff v. Society of New York Hospitals, 211 N.Y. 125, 129-130 (1914).

387. Schmitt v. Pierce, 344 S.W.2d 120 (1961).

388. Scott Deveau, Jing Cao, *Microsoft Apologizes After Twitter Chat Bot Experiment Goes Awry,* BLOOMBERG, (Mar. 25, 2016, 04:31 PM), https://www.bloomberg.com/news/articles/2016-03-25/microsoft-apologizes-after-twitter-chat-bot-experiment-goes-awry?in_source=embedded-checkout-banner.

389. Sean M., Stephen J., *Freedom of Conscience in Healthcare: Distinctions and Limits,* 10 J Bioeth Inq. 347, 347-354 (2013).

390. Seifert, Josef, *Is Brain Death Actually Death?,* 76 The Monist 175, 176 (1993).

391. Shah S.K., Robert Truog, et al., Death and Legal Fictions 37 J Med Ethics 719, 719-722 (2011).

392. Shania Kennedy, *AI in Medical Imaging May Amplify Biases, Inequities,* HEALTH IT ANALYTICS, (May 3, 2023), https://healthitanalytics.com/news/ai-in-medical-imaging-may-amplify-biases-inequities.

A. Sharif, Moorlock G., *Influencing Relatives to Respect Donor Autonomy: Should We Nudge Families to Consent to Organ Donation?,* 32 Bioethics 155, 156-163 (2017).

393. Shewmon D.A., *Brain Death: A Conclusion in Search of a Justification,* 48 Hastings Cent Rep. S22, S22-S25 (2018).

394. Shewmon D.A., *Truly Reconciling the Case of Jahi McMath,* 29 Neurocrit Care 165, 165-170 (2018).

395. Shewmon DA, Salamon N., *The Extraordinary Case of Jahi McMath*, 64 Perspect Biol Med. 457, 457-478 (2021).

396. Shewmon, D.A., *Chronic Brain Death*, 51 Neurol. 1538, 1538-1539 (1998).

397. Sibley, W.M., *The Rational versus the Reasonable*, 62 The Phil. Rev. 554, 554-560 (1953).

398. Siminoff L.A., Burant C., et al., *Death and Organ Procurement: Public Beliefs and Attitudes*, 59 Soc Sci Med. 2325, 2325-2334 (2004).

399. Siobhan McAndrew, *The Contested Death of Aden Hailu*, RENO GAZETTE-J (Mar. 25, 2016), http://www.rgj.com/story/news/2016/03/25/contested-death-aden-hailu/.

400. Smith M., *Brain Death: Time for an International Consensus*, 108 BJA i6, i7 (2012).

401. Sonali Vadi, Sunil Shroff, *Redefining Death: Urgent Need to Evolve Toward a Homogenous Definition of Death in India*, 10 IJCCC 368, 368-369 (2019).

402. Sri Sunarti, Ferry F. Rahman, et al., *Artificial Intelligence in Healthcare: Opportunities and Risk for Future*, 35 Gaceta Sanitaria S67, S68-S70 (2021).

403. St. John W., *The Irish Patient and Dr. Lawsuit*, N.Y. TIMES (Apr. 24, 2005), https://www.nytimes.com/2005/04/24/fashion/sundaystyles/the-irish-patient-and-dr-lawsuit.html.

404. Stanley v. Schriro, 598 F.3d 612, 615 (9th Cir. 2010)

405. State of Andhra Pradesh v. P. Laxmi Devi & Others (Writ Petition No. 12649 of 2000) (Ind.).

406. State of Karnataka v. Union of India & Anr. (1978) 2 SCR 1. (Ind.).

407. State of Rajasthan v. Union of India, 1984 SCC (2) 292 (Ind.).

408. State of West Bengal v. Union of India, 1964 SCR (1) 371 (Ind.).

409. State v. Olson, 435 N.W.2d 530 (1989).

410. Steinback R.L., *Mainstream Science is Frosty Over Keeping the Dead on Ice,* CHICAGO TRIBUNE, (Jul. 17, 2019, 12:00 AM), https://www.chicagotribune.com/news/ct-xpm-2002-09-29-0209290429-story.html.

411. Stephen Weng, Luiz Vaz, et al., *Prediction of Premature All-Cause Mortality: A Prospective General Population Cohort Study Comparing Machine-Learning and Standard Epidemiological Approaches,* 14 PLos One e0214365 (2019).

412. Steven House, Caroline Schoo, et al., Advance Directives, STATPEARLS (Jan. 20, 2023), https://www.ncbi.nlm.nih.gov/books/NBK459133/.

413. Stormans, Inc. v. Selecky, 844 F.Supp. 2d 1172 (2015).

414. STUP. R., STANDARD OPERATING PROCEDURES: A WRITING GUIDE (2001).

415. SUSHRUTA SAMHITA (V.J. Trikamji ed. 2014) (originally written by Sushruta, who is considered to be the father of Surgery).

416. Swash, M., et al., *Brain Death: Still-Unresolved Issues Worldwide,* 58 Neurol. 9, 9-10 (2002).

417. Syndicat Northcrest v. Amselem, 2 SCR 551 (2004) (Can.).

418. THE CONSTITUTION OF INDIA, 1950, Part XI.

419. THE GAZETTE OF INDIA: EXTRAORDINARY (1995), https://notto.gov.in/WriteReadData/Portal/images/THOA-Rules-2014.pdf (Forms 8 and 10).

420. THE PRESIDENT'S COUNCIL ON BIOETHICS, CONTROVERSIES IN THE DETERMINATION OF DEATH: A WHITE PAPER (2008).

421. Thomas Davenport, John Glaser, *Just-in-Time Delivery Comes to Knowledge Management,* 80 Harv Bus Rev. 107, 107-111 (2002).

422. Thomas Davenport, Ravi Kalakota, *The Potential for Artificial Intelligence in Healthcare,* 6 Future Healthc J. 94, 94 (2019).

423. Thomas v. Anderson, 96 Cal. App. 2d 371 (1950).

424. Thomas v. Review Board of Indiana Employment Security Division, 450 U.S. 707, 718 (1981).

425. Tom Dart, *Texas Hospital Acknowledges Brain Dead Status of Pregnant Woman*, THE GUARDIAN (Jan. 24, 2014, 4:43 PM), https://www.theguardian.com/world/2014/jan/24/texas-hospital-acknowledges-brain-dead-pregnant-woman.

426. Tucker v. Lower, 1 Va. Cir. 124 (1972).

427. U.S. DEPARTMENT OF HEALTH AND HUMAN SERVICES, CONSCIENCE AND RELIGIOUS NON-DISCRIMINATION (2022).

428. ULC, UNIFORM DETERMINATION OF DEATH ACT (1981).

429. UNIFORM LAW COMMISSION, SESSION RESOURCES (2023) (on file with the author).

430. United Nations Declaration on Human Rights, G.A. Res. 217A (III) (UDHR), Dec. 10, 1948, art. 18.

431. UNITED NATIONS HUMAN RIGHTS OFFICE OF THE HIGH COMMISSIONER, #FAITH4RIGHTS TOOLKIT (2022).

432. UNITED NATIONS STATISTICS DIVISION, https://unstats.un.org/UNSDWebsite/ (last visited Jan. 18, 2023).

433. United States v. Seeger, 380 U.S. 163 (1965).

434. University Health Services v. Piazzi, Richmond County No. CV86-RCCV-464 (1986).

435. *Use of AI in Healthcare and Medicine is Booming – Here's How the Medical Field is Benefiting from AI in 2021 and Beyond,* INSIDER, (Jan. 11, 2023), https://www.insiderintelligence.com/insights/artificial-intelligence-healthcare/.

436. Vacco v. Quill, 521 U.S. 793 (1997).

437. VAUGHN L., BIOETHICS: PRINCIPLES, ISSUES AND CASES (1st ed. 2016).

438. Veith, Fein, Tendler, et al., *Brain Death – Part II: A Status Report of Legal Considerations,* 238 JAMA, 1744, 1745 (1977).

439. Verheijde, L. Joseph, Rady, Y. Mohamed, et al., *Neuroscience and Brain Death Controversies: The Elephant in the Room,* 57 J. Relig. Health 1745, 1746 (2018).

440. Vincent Triola, *Differences Between Virtue, Utilitarianism and Deontological Ethics,* VINCENT TRIOLA (Mar. 25, 2021), https://vincenttriola.com/blogs/ten-years-of-academic-writing/what-are-the-differences-between-virtue-utilitarianism-deontological-ethics.

441. VIRGINIA EUBANKS, AUTOMATING INEQUALITY (St. Martin's Press, 2018).

442. Walker, A.E., *Cerebral Death, in* 2 THE CLINICAL NEUROSCIENCES 75, 75-89 (Chase T.N. ed., 1975).

443. Weinstock D., *Conscientious Refusal and Healthcare Professionals: Does Religion Make a Difference?* 28 Bioethics 8, 8-15 (2014).

444. West-Oram P, Buyx A., *Conscientious Objection in Healthcare Provision: A New Dimension,* 30 Bioethics 336, 336-343 (2016).

445. Whetstine L. Streat S., et al., *Pro/Con Ethics Debate: When is Dead Really Dead,* 9 Critical Care 538, 538-540 (2005).

446. WICCLAIR M., CONSCIENTIOUS OBJECTION IN HEALTHCARE: AN ETHICAL ANALYSIS, (1st ed. 2011).

447. Wijdicks, E.F.M., *Brain Death Worldwide: Accepted Fact but No Global Consensus in Diagnostic Criteria,* 58 Neurol. 20, 23 (2002).

448. Wikler, D. et al., *Editorial,* 261 JAMA 2246, 2247 (1989).

449. Winkfield v. Children's Hospital Oakland, (N.D. Cal. Jan 22. 2014).

450. Winston Chiong, *Brain Death Without Definitions,* 35 Hastings Cent Rep 20, 21 (2005).

451. Wong L.P., *Factors Limiting Deceased Organ Donation: Focus Groups' Perspective from Culturally Diverse Community,* 42 Transplant Proc 1439, 1439-1444 (2010).

452. XAVIER BICHAT, PHYSIOLOGICAL RESEARCH ON LIFE AND DEATH (Tobias Watkins trans., Smith & Maxwell 1809) (1799).

453. Y.N. Nuraliev, *Doctor's Ethics in Ancient East Written Classics and in the Works of Middle Age Medical Scientists* in 2 INTERACTIONS BETWEEN INDIAN AND CENTRAL ASIAN SCIENCE AND TECHNOLOGY IN MEDIEVAL TIMES 11-8 (W.H. Abdi, M.S. Asimov, et.al. eds., 1990).

454. Yang Q., Fan Y., et al., *Acceptance in Theory but not Practice: Chinese Medical Providers' Perception of Brain Death,* 8 Neuroethics, 299, 299-313 (2015).

455. Yang, Qing, and Geoffrey Miller, *East–west differences in Perception of Brain Death: Review of History, Current Understandings and Directions for Future Research* 8 JBI (2014).

456. Yossi N., *Religious Conscientious Exemptions,* 30 Law Philos. 143, 143-166 (2011).

457. Youngner S.J., Landefeld C.S., et al. *Brain Death and Organ Retrieval: A Cross-Sectional Survey of Knowledge and Concepts among Health Professionals,* 15 JAMA 2205, 2206-2208 (1989).

458. Yu B., Beam A., *Artificial Intelligence in Healthcare,* 2 Nature Biomed Eng. 719, 719-721 (2018).

459. Zaidani Attamimi, Hafizuddin Awang, et. al., *Challenges and Barriers of Brain Death Reporting in Malaysia,* 8 IJPHCS 87, 95 (2021).

460. Zuckerman S., Gerrit K., et al., *Surprising Pandemic Experiences: A Confrontation Between Principle-Based and Virtue Ethics, and A Plea for Virtue Ethics Training for Medical Students and Residents,* 1 J. Eval Clin Pract. 1, 1-8 (2023).

www.ingramcontent.com/pod-product-compliance
Lightning Source LLC
La Vergne TN
LVHW051051210926
848486LV00002B/66
* 9 7 9 8 8 9 6 1 0 3 2 9 5 *